You CAN Talk to
Your Animals

You CAN Talk to Your Animals

Animal Communicators Tell You How

Janine Adams

HOWELL
BOOK
HOUSE

A Division of

An   ny
Foster City, CA   New York, NY

3 3305 01411 5012

Howell Book House

IDG Books Worldwide, Inc.

An International Data Group Company

919 E. Hillsdale Boulevard

Suite 400

Foster City, CA 94404

ISBN 1-58245-177-X

Manufactured in the United States of America

10 9 8 7 6 5 4 3 2 1

Parts of this book, in a slightly different form, first appeared in *Pets: part of the family* magazine, March/April 1999.

Material from the following books has been used with permission:

Animal Talk: Interspecies Telepathic Communication, by Penelope Smith. Beyond Words Publishing, 1999.

Conversations with Animals: Cherished Messages and Memories as Told by an Animal Communicator, by Lydia Hiby with Bonnie S. Weintraub. NewSage Press, 1998.

Talking with the Animals, by Patty Summers. Hampton Roads Publishing Company, 1998.

What the Animals Tell Me: Understanding Your Pet's Complex Emotions, by Sonya Fitzpatrick with Patricia Burkhart Smith. Hyperion, 1997.

Dedication

*To Kramer and Scout, without whom
this book would not have been written.*

Acknowledgements

Researching and writing this book has been an enriching journey for me, due largely to the wonderful people I had the opportunity to interview. It was a pleasure talking with people who are so connected to their animals.

I'd like to thank all the communicators who so generously shared information with me in the spirit of spreading the word about animal communication as far and wide as possible. In particular, Ginny Debbink and Gail De Sciose who spent hours with me and tolerated my incessant questions. Thank you.

I also owe a debt of gratitude to the clients of the animal communicators who shared their stories with me. They often spoke through tears, but to a person they were enthusiastic about sharing their experiences so that others might be exposed to the wonders of animal communication.

Thank you as well to Dominique De Vito, publisher at Howell Book House, who invited me to write this book. I'll always be grateful to her for taking a chance on me. And many thanks to Nikki Moustaki, Kira Sexton and Amanda Pisani, my editors at Howell.

And, finally, thanks to the animals who so generously share their wisdom when asked, especially my dogs, Kramer and Scout, who are the lights of my life. A very special thanks to my husband, Barry Marcus, who supports me in everything I do.

Contents

Contents

Introduction

I know what you're thinking. The idea that someone can speak telepathically with your animal companion—and not even be anywhere near him, let alone in the same room—seems far-fetched. As consumers, we're always on the lookout for fraudulent claims. This one waves a giant red flag; it flies in the face of what most of us were raised to believe.

When I first heard about telepathic animal communication four years ago, I scoffed at the idea. Lydia Hiby, a communicator I subsequently interviewed for this book, was coming to St. Louis, where I lived at the time. There was a notice about her lecture and private consultations at the dog-training club where my Standard Poodle, Kramer, and I attended classes. As a freelance writer, I was hot to write a magazine article debunking her claims. I figured I knew everything that had gone on in Kramer's life since he was nine weeks old. It would be easy for me to trip her up.

Somehow I never got an assignment to write about Lydia (in fact her visit was canceled), so I never had my chance to be an anti-animal communication muckraker.

What a difference a few years makes.

Just two years later, I found myself hiring an animal communicator to talk with my two Standard Poodles (Scout joined our family in

1996). I approached the session with an open mind and had excellent results. Why the change? The communicator, Ginny Debbink, was an Internet friend I'd known for a few years without knowing that she could communicate telepathically with animals. Other Internet friends (all of whom, including Ginny, participated in a particular Internet mailing list for dog lovers) started telling me about their experiences using Ginny's services. I was intrigued. After I heard their stories, animal communication didn't sound so outlandish.

I knew Ginny to be a knowledgeable, caring person who was very generous with information and I trusted that she wasn't out to cheat me. Thus I passed a huge hurdle—the fear that a "psychic" was trying to make a sucker out of me.

I eagerly anticipated our first session, in which I would speak to Ginny over the phone, wait while she relayed my questions telepathically to Kramer and Scout, and listen while she interpreted their responses for me. I wasn't disappointed. That first session gave me fresh insights into my dogs—companions I thought I knew so well. Those insights (and others gained from subsequent sessions) are mentioned throughout the chapters of this book. But suffice it to say they've helped me tackle some behavior problems, helped me understand Kramer and Scout better, and made me feel closer than ever to them.

When that first session was over, I felt exhilarated. It was as if a window into my dogs' world had been opened up for me. A whole new way of relating to my dogs was available—one that I, like most people who live with animals, had yearned for. I could actually have a two-way conversation with them!

At first I was very cautious about telling others about my animal communication session. I think I was worried that they would think I was a crackpot. But as I started talking about it, I discovered that many of my dog friends had used an animal communicator—people I never would have guessed as being open to it. And while I'm still sometimes met with disbelief when I introduce the subject of animal communication (some people simply refuse to consider the possibility), once

I start talking about my own experiences and those of others I've spoken with, I find that people are eager to learn more.

Dawn Hayman, another communicator I interviewed for this book, says that in 1987 when she began working as an animal communicator, the subject was really taboo. But in the last five years or so, it has really grown in popularity and acceptance. "People are more open to this now," she says.

I'm hoping you will be interested and open too. My goal for this book is to explore animal communication with readers so that they will consider the possibility. Each chapter will show you how animal communication—whether performed by a professional communicator, a skilled friend, or you—can help you in various aspects of your life with your animal companion(s). Using information supplied by animal communicators, plus the actual experiences of animal lovers who have used the services of professional communicators, I will show you how animal communication has helped others, and how it can help you.

And then I will show you how you can do it yourself. Animal communicators believe that everyone has the innate ability to communicate telepathically with animals. It's a matter of opening your mind and your heart to it and practicing some simple techniques. Many of us probably communicated with animals as children, but we shut off that ability after being told it was only our "imagination." At the end of this book you will find some step-by-step approaches to learning to tap into your inner ability to communicate with animals again.

Receiving telepathic messages from animals comes easier to some people than others. I've attended two workshops, both of which were helpful, and I've had the opportunity to talk with nearly a dozen communicators. Yet my own skills are still in the very early stages. Animal communication takes practice and a quiet mind, both of which are hard to come by in this fast-paced life. If you're interested, a workshop can be a great way to start out. But if that's not possible, the techniques outlined in this book should help you get started.

For those readers who are new to animal communication and are perhaps doubting whether it could possibly be real, I'm hoping this book will allow you to open yourself up to it and explore the ways that animal communication can help you and your animal friends. Once you've experienced what animal communication can offer, you just might wonder why you were ever so skeptical.

For those of you who have already experienced the benefits of telepathic animal communication, I hope this book will provide you with even more ways that animal communication can help you. I've found it immensely rewarding talking with the dozens of people I interviewed for this book. I hope you will find their stories beneficial as well.

A few words about language. The more I researched this book, the less appropriate the word "owner" seemed to be to describe the relationship between human and animal companions. "A dog calls his human companion his 'person' not his 'owner'," says Dawn Hayman. Similarly, "pet" describes a subservience that many animals reveal they don't possess.

So in this book, you'll see the terms "person," or "human" or "human companion" rather than "owner." And I've used "animal friend" or "animal" or "animal companion" rather than "pet."

When it comes to gender, professional animal communicators are overwhelmingly women, so when a generic pronoun is needed, I've elected to use the word "she." With the animals, I've applied "he" or "she" at random, to avoid the awkwardness of "he or she." Under no circumstances does the word "it" come into play when referring to an animal in this book!

Chapter 1

What Is Animal Communication?

···

If you speak out loud to your animal friend, you communicate telepathically with him. We communicate telepathically with our animals all the time. Telepathy is simply the pictures and feelings behind the words we speak, says animal communicator Dawn Hayman. Every time we speak, we send a telepathic message. Animals are open to receiving telepathic messages, whereas we humans, who rely on spoken language, have closed off those channels.

"So when we speak to our animals, we send telepathic messages that they receive. In return, our animals send us telepathic messages as well," says Dawn. The purpose of this book is to help you learn how to open yourself up to receiving those telepathic messages—and how to trust them.

When we were kids, our telepathic channels hadn't been blocked. Human children talk to animals all the time. But when those conversations are reported to their parents, they're invalidated. Adults are always dismissing kids' musings, telling them, "It's just your imagination."

I know when I was in elementary school I'd come home from school late and be met by my frantic mother. Invariably, I was late because I'd stop to talk with a cat. I honestly don't recall whether I'd had two-way conversations with the neighborhood cats (if I did, it wasn't remarkable to me), but I do vividly recall being told every day as I left for school, "Don't stop to talk to any cats!"

If you think back, you might recall similar conversations with animals. As adults, we have to work hard to open the door to inner telepathic abilities that were slammed shut for us when we were young.

ARE ANIMALS PSYCHIC?

The whole concept of animal communication is met with skepticism by the scientifically minded who require "proof" before recognizing that something is real. Anecdotal evidence isn't good enough. But just because something hasn't been scientifically proven doesn't mean it doesn't exist. When I hear convincing stories from people I trust, it's enough for me to at least accept the possibility that something like telepathic communication with animals might exist.

Communicator Ginny Debbink likens the energy used to communicate telepathically (which she calls "the energy of love") to electricity. Centuries ago, humans didn't know about electricity or how to use it. But electricity was still there, waiting to be harnessed. "We don't know everything that is around us," she says. "I don't really understand electricity. I just use it." Ginny feels the same way about animal communication.

Underlying some of the skepticism about animal communication is the question of whether animals are capable of thoughts and emotions. If they're not—as some scientists still insist even in the 21st century—then clearly animals wouldn't be very good conversationalists. In order to accept animal communication, you must accept that animals have something to communicate.

"I think it is egocentric to think that only humans have feelings and emotions," says communicator Gail De Sciose. As someone who has spoken with literally thousands of animals, Gail is comfortable in the knowledge that animals are of the same spirit and same consciousness as humans.

In his recent book *Dogs That Know When Their Owners Are Coming Home,* British scientist Rupert Sheldrake sets out to scientifically document that animals have psychic powers.

He surveyed people who work with animals and learned of 2,200 cases of unexplained perceptiveness in animals. He conducted random surveys of households in England and the United States and found that about 50 percent of those surveyed believed that their dogs were telepathic and about 35 percent believed that to be true of their cats. (I guess skepticism isn't as widespread as I had thought.) And then he conducted controlled experiments of 250 dogs, videotaping them and asking their people to arrive home at randomly varying times. He found that many dogs know in advance when their humans are on the way home.

When we talked about that book, animal communicator Lydia Hiby provided an explanation for the phenomenon of dogs knowing in advance when their people were heading home. When you think about going home and anticipate seeing your animal friend, Lydia says, you send your dog a telepathic message. He knows you're on the way home. It's as simple as that.

I applaud Sheldrake's scientific scrutiny. But for me, it's not necessary. After having spoken with nearly a dozen animal communicators and dozens of their clients, I have no problem accepting the notion that animals communicate telepathically with us and with one another. I also accept that we all have the ability to tune in telepathically with our animals (though some people find it easier to do than others), and that doing so will be to the benefit of both animal and human.

WE'RE ALL ASPIRING DR. DOLITTLES

Everyone who lives with animals has undoubtedly, at one time or another, wished that they knew what their animal friends were thinking.

That's why animal communication captures the imagination of animal lovers who hear about it. Animal communicator Sonya Fitzpatrick is a regular guest on a radio show in Houston. During her guest appearances, she talks with people's animals on the air. After her appearances, listeners line up outside the radio station, she says, hoping that Sonya will be able to talk with their animals.

When animal communicator Nancy Wallace is a guest on "Pet Central," a radio show on WGN in Chicago hosted by Steve Dale, the phone lines are always jammed. "People are desperate to know what their pets are really thinking," explains Steve. "The question the listeners ask Nancy most often: 'Is my Fido or Fluffy happy?' People call who don't typically believe in psychics or mind reading or any of that, and they haven't had readings ever in their lives for themselves—but this illustrates just how much they yearn for a peek inside their pet's psyche."

I can understand the fascination. Animal communication was nothing short of a revelation for me. It's given me the opportunity to talk with beloved family members who previously had communicated only the most basic information to me (rather, I understood only the most basic of what they communicated to me).

Now that I've been exposed to it, I think everyone could benefit from either consulting with a professional animal communicator or learning to do it themselves. Regular animal communication sessions are now a part of how I care for my two Standard Poodles, Kramer and Scout.

ARE ANIMAL COMMUNICATORS PSYCHICS?

"Telepathy is not mind reading," says Dawn Hayman. Like any conversation, it's a two-way street. There must be both a sender and a receiver.

Rightly or wrongly, the term "psychic" has in our culture a subtle subtext that, for me anyway, waves a red flag with the word "fraud" emblazoned on it. The term "animal communicator" is preferred to the seemingly more pejorative "pet psychic." It's not necessarily a fear of people's reactions to the term "psychic" but rather an interest in accuracy that leads most animal communicators to call themselves communicators rather than psychics. Most aren't psychic; they don't predict the future. They simply relay communication from animals.

That said, "animal communicator" and "psychic" aren't mutually exclusive terms. Most of the communicators I interviewed for this book aren't clairvoyant. But at least one, Sonya Fitzpatrick, is. "I feel that my clairvoyant ability really helps my animal communication work," Sonya says. "I get things very quickly."

TELEPATHIC COMMUNICATION BETWEEN HUMANS

Several of the animal communicators I interviewed work with humans as well. Sonya Fitzpatrick has begun communicating with autistic people in much the same manner that she communicates with animals. This proved to be immensely helpful for her first such client, whose adult child is autistic and therefore unable to express her thoughts aloud. The autistic person had been labeled mentally retarded, but Sonya discovered that she was quite mentally alert, she just couldn't express her thoughts.

"Autistic children speak telepathically, just like animals do," says Sonya. The autistic person relayed information about occurrences in her family's life that her mother had not been sure she'd understood. "The mother never stopped crying during the first session," recalls Sonya. She now speaks with her daughter, through Sonya, on a regular basis and has referred other parents of autistic people to Sonya.

Sonya isn't alone in working with humans as well as animals. Other communicators I interviewed, including Sharon Callahan and Alice McClure, work with humans too.

THE ANIMAL COMMUNICATORS

When Penelope Smith started her career as an animal communicator in the mid-1970s, there were "about two" professional animal communicators working, she told me. Today, according to Penelope, there are between 100 and 200 professional animal communicators working in this country.

I interviewed 11 of them for this book. Each was extremely generous with sharing information on how they do it, how you can do it, and how animal communication benefits both animals and humans (including animal communicators). Brief biographical sketches of each (arranged alphabetically) are included here and contact information is presented in the Appendix A, "Resources."

Sharon Callahan

Sharon Callahan is a writer, photographer, flower essence practitioner and internationally recognized animal communication specialist. She is a leading pioneer in the use of flower essences in the treatment of animals and her books on the topic are the first in their field. Sharon's many articles on animals, flower essences and spirituality appear in publications worldwide.

After a near-death experience in 1988, Sharon restructured her life to include more time for spirituality, friendship and communion with nature and animals. This experience enhanced her ability to communicate with animals telepathically and inspired her to create Anaflora, original flower essences and flower essence formulas designed specifically for animals. In her work, Sharon combines telepathic communication skills with an uncanny ability to select the appropriate healing essences for each animal. Connecting with the soul of the animal, she offers diagnostic insight, inspiration and guidance. She draws on a repertoire of hundreds of flower essences that she makes herself in Mt. Shasta, California, where she has lived for the past 20 years.

Sharon brings to her practice a background in the human medical setting, including psychiatric clinics, the treatment of children with disabilities, grief therapy and suicide counseling. Today, her expertise in the fields of animal communication and flower essence therapy has gained the respect not only of individuals, but also of animal welfare organizations, shelters, veterinarians and flower essence professionals throughout the world.

Anita Curtis

Anita Curtis has been a practicing animal communicator since 1992. This is her second career; she worked in the accounting department of the Prudential Life Insurance company prior to early retirement in 1994.

Anita originally studied communications with Jeri Ryan, an associate of Penelope Smith. She has taken numerous courses and workshops taught by Penelope in California and New York. She continues to grow in her communications knowledge and skills.

Anita is the author of *Animal Wisdom: How to Hear the Animals* (i Universe, 2000). In addition to her private consultations, Anita teaches animal communication workshops, lectures and writes a newsletter, *Animal Channel*. She has been on radio and television and has been featured in numerous magazine and newspaper articles. She enjoys teaching and donates part of her workshop proceeds to several animal-related charities. She feels a strong responsibility to return something to the animals who have given her so much.

Ginny Debbink

Ginny Debbink graduated from Drew University in 1974, with a bachelor's degree in anthropology. She has been working with animals her entire life. Since 1977 she has been training dogs and breeding and exhibiting German Shepherd Dogs. In 1990, after her first consultation with an animal communicator, she began exploring her own abilities in this field.

After several years of working and practicing with friends' animals, and at the insistent urging of many of those same friends, Ginny began to take clients, and became a professional animal communicator in 1995. Among her regular clients are my Standard Poodles, Kramer and Scout.

Currently, she and her husband share their lives and home with a German Shepherd, a retired racing Greyhound, a Shih Tzu rescued after her owner's death, a Yellow Nape Amazon Parrot, and a Grey Cockatiel.

Ginny's work with Kramer and Scout provided the inspiration for my article about animal communication in the March/April 1999 issue of *Pets: part of the family* magazine, which in turn inspired the writing and publication of this book.

Gail De Sciose

Gail De Sciose is a counselor who communicates directly with animals. She holds a bachelor of science in education and a master of science in education and counseling. In 1979, she began to practice meditation. She believes that her ability to quiet her own thoughts enables her to hear the voices and wisdom of the animals.

Gail participates in ongoing studies with various practitioners of the healing arts. She holds certification in first and second degree Reiki (Reiki is a hands-on healing technique that uses universal life force energy), and is continuing her training in the areas of animal nutrition, behavior, holistic health care and alternative healing modalities. Gail is committed to promoting greater understanding and respect between humans and other beings.

Gail gives lectures and teaches classes on the subject of animal communication. She has been interviewed for radio and television programs, as well as for books, and newspaper and magazine articles.

Most of her communication sessions are performed long distance by telephone or letter. Gail has clients all over the United States and the world.

Sonya Fitzpatrick

Sonya "Sunny" Fitzpatrick was born in central England and grew up in a quiet, rural setting where she acquired a deep love for all animals. At the age of 17, Sonya left home to pursue a career in fashion and modeling in London. During this period she worked in all the major fashion capitals of Europe, appearing frequently on television, and modeled for many noted designers, including Norman Hartwell, couturier to Queen Elizabeth.

Sonya moved to Houston in 1991 to establish an etiquette business. She is a consultant to several major corporations, including Continental Airlines, and many of Houston's most prominent families in matters of social and business etiquette.

As an animal communicator, she is a regular guest on phone-in radio talk shows in Houston and Dallas, where she helps countless people solve their pet problems. Her clientele has expanded to include animal lovers from all over the world, who consult her regularly concerning health and behavioral problems with their animals. She is also a popular speaker and regularly gives seminars on animal behavior and healing throughout the country. In 1996, Sonya was featured in a nationally broadcast HBO documentary film exploring the relationship between humans and animals.

She is the author, with Patricia Burkhart Smith, of *What the Animals Tell Me* (Hyperion, 1997).

Dawn Hayman

Dawn Hayman has been communicating with animals since childhood and she has been doing professional consultations with people and their animal companions since 1990. She has worked with renowned animal communicator Penelope Smith and with many veterinarians to expand her knowledge, and has been a TTEAM practitioner. (TTEAM is a holistic method of training, healing and overcoming problem behavior in horses.) Additionally, her extensive hands-on experience with the many species of animals at her animal sanctuary, Spring Farm CARES, and a Bachelor's degree in social work, have well prepared Dawn to assist her clients with the varied situations they encounter with their animals.

Dawn has thousands of clients from all 50 states, Canada, Europe and even Saudi Arabia. Her clients range from lay people, just wanting to better understand their animal friends, to trainers, veterinarians, holistic practitioners and top-level performers in the animal world. In addition to consulting, she lectures and gives workshops on inter-species communication.

Dawn is cofounder and Assistant Director of Spring Farm CARES, a nonprofit sanctuary for domestic animals and the world's first center for the teaching of interspecies communication. All proceeds from consultations, lectures and workshops go directly to Spring Farm CARES, which cares for over 200 animals, including horses, ponies, goats, sheep, llamas, cats, dogs, rabbits, ducks, chickens and other birds.

Lydia Hiby

Lydia Hiby has worked as an animal communicator since 1982. The co-author (with Bonnie S. Weintraub) of *Conversations with Animals* (NewSage Press, 1998), she has communicated with thousands of animals and their people seeking a higher level of understanding in their relationships. Lydia graduated from the Agriculture College in Delhi, New York with a degree in animal science and has worked with several animal clinics as a veterinarian's assistant. She has a national following for her work as an animal communicator, and has received extensive media attention because of her accuracy and success in talking with animals from many different species. Lydia has been featured on *Leeza, 48 Hours, Late Night with David Letterman,* and numerous other television and radio shows. Her work has been covered by many newspapers, including *The Washington Post,* the *Los Angeles Times*, the *Chicago Tribune*, and *USA Today.*

Lydia lives in Southern California with her animal family. She gives lectures and seminars, holds in-person meetings with large groups of animals and people as well as individual phone consultations.

Alice McClure

Alice McClure grew up in Brooklyn, New York. As a child she began having experiences that raised many of the questions she has been pursuing throughout her life. While in her early twenties, fortune brought her together with Willem Nyland, the practical spirituality ideas of Gurdjieff and, later on, Sun Bear, a Chippewa medicine man. In Sun Bear's company Alice finally felt at home with her intuition.

Alice has been involved with energy medicine and healing for 30 years but it wasn't until her young daughter's near death in 1982 that her intuitive work kicked into high gear. Again grand fortune/ synchronicity brought Alice together with a special person, the

Reverend Thelma Meites, who could help her order, refine and direct the mystical experiences she started having as a child.

Alice is blessed to be living with her astronomer husband Bruce, her children, Jack Russell Terriers, horses and cats on a farm in a remote part of northern New York. She is also a lay naturopath and often blends intuitive and practical advice. When not working with animals and their people, Alice McClure is a part-time middle school teacher.

Nancy Mueller

Nancy Mueller was born and raised in New Jersey and has spent most of her life caring for and about animals, particularly horses. She began riding horses at the Watchung Stables, a county facility, as soon as she was old enough to qualify—age eight. She was given her first horse at age 13, and has had a horse or horses in her care ever since. She had a very successful hunter/jumper show career, as Nancy Kaiser, from 1965 to 1975.

Nancy entered the University of North Carolina in 1969. She transferred from the UNC School of Pharmacy to one at Rutgers University in 1973. In 1975, she graduated, with highest honors, from Rutgers University's College of Pharmacy.

In 1977, Nancy married Robert Mueller, D.V.M., her horse's veterinarian. She left the practice of pharmacy to help run her husband's veterinary practice, equine hospital, and farm. From 1980 to 1985, she helped run a thoroughbred breeding business with her husband at their Fair Chance Farm. During this time they were confronted with many challenging medical cases—most with successful outcomes, but not all. Their losses took a heavy personal toll on them both. In 1985, they decided to leave the thoroughbred breeding business to others.

In 1993, with the help of one of her husband's patients, Nancy reawakened to her skills of telepathic animal communication. She spent 18 months working with many wonderful animals, and one gifted person, who helped her develop her skills once again. Over time, through the needs of her animal patients, Nancy has been introduced to new concepts of healing. Nancy is a certified consultant for the Spiritual Response Association. She combines spiritual response therapy, vibrational remedies (flower essences, gem elixirs, color and light therapies), and shamanic healing with her animal communication skills. Her clients receive not just understanding, but solutions to their specific problems; be they physical, mental, emotional and/or spiritual. Healing for the entire being!

Nancy is dedicated to bridging the chasm that has developed between people and their animals. "An improved understanding between species will enrich the lives of all involved," Nancy firmly believes. "We are all teachers; we are all students! This is our reason for being here in this life."

Penelope Smith

Penelope Smith is a pioneer in the practice of interspecies telepathic communication and has become the world's foremost teacher of basic and advanced courses in this field. In this capacity, she has helped launch the careers of numerous professional animal communicators.

Having communicated with animals throughout her life, Penelope discovered in 1981 that animals could be relieved of emotional traumas and other problems through the same counseling techniques that benefit humans. Contributing to her success are her degrees in the social sciences; years of training and experience in human counseling, nutrition and holistic energy balancing methods; research into animal nutrition, anatomy, behavior and care; and the firsthand education gathered from the thousands of animals she has contacted. The author of numerous magazine articles and books, including *Animal Talk* (Beyond Words Publishing, 1999) and *When Animals Speak* (Beyond Words Publishing, 1999), Penelope has also created audio and videotapes. She publishes a quarterly journal, *Species Link,* and is an internationally known lecturer and workshop leader.

Penelope feels that the sacred connection we make with other species through telepathic communication is essential for human wholeness. She believes that everyone is born with the power to communicate with other species; although most people have put aside and forgotten this gift, it can be reclaimed for the benefit of all beings on Earth. She lives with members of her animal family in the woods of northern California.

Patty Summers

Since she was a child, Patty Summers has talked with the animals—always knowing that her true path was to work with them. She has worked professionally with animals since 1985, in veterinary practices, as a manager of pet supply stores, as an animal control officer and at the local humane society.

Patty has received training in the Tellington T-Touch technique (a massage method using circular touch to reduce tension and change behavior in dogs, cats and other animals) and is a certified Reiki practitioner. She has also studied and incorporated numerous behavioral and healing techniques into her practice. She currently provides communication workshops as well as consultations for domestic animals and their human companions to resolve conflicts or to aid in communication.

In her book *Talking with the Animals* (Hampton Roads Publishing Co., 1998), Patty shared her knowledge and experience with the world, but she insists that she is only a messenger. "*Talking with the Animals* is *their* gift of wisdom and insights," she says.

STILL A SKEPTIC?

As you can see, the professional animal communicators I spoke with have studied many aspects of animal behavior, health and healing. They did not just decide to make a buck by hanging out a shingle in Greenwich Village. These people have made a commitment to finding and using their telepathic abilities. Read on to learn more about their experiences—and how you, too, can talk to the animals.

Chapter 2

How Do Animal Communicators Do It?

....

Animal communicators will tell you that they're not special, that they don't possess unique powers. In fact, they say, we all have the ability to communicate with animals.

But professional animal communicators have worked hard to hone those abilities. Through all their practice and training, they've evolved to a point where they can actually inhabit the body of the animals with whom they're speaking. They can see through the animal's eyes, if they desire. And since they do it all the time, they can do it with speed and ease.

So if we can all do it, why is there a need for the professional communicator? Like everything else, animal communication takes practice. Lots of practice. And it also requires trust. If we can't get instant validation of what we've received from the animals, it's hard to trust that we didn't just make it up.

If you hire a professional whose skills you trust, your own self-doubt won't come into play. In addition, if you're looking to address a problem or issue with an emotional component, it's nice to have an objective third party act as an intermediary between you and your animal. In fact, many communicators will hire another communicator to speak with their own animals if an issue needs discussing where emotions run high. "Many animal communicators get another professional to check on their communications with their own animals," says Patty Summers.

Many professional animal communicators bring more to the table than an ability to communicate telepathically. Although most describe themselves as a conduit, they also act as counselors, helping you resolve problems with your animals. They can be skilled mediators. Sometimes you'll have to negotiate a compromise with your animal in order to change a problem behavior. And many such professionals are trained in, or have a close familiarity with, healing techniques that go beyond animal communication. They can often advise you in seeking other ways to help your animal friends.

It's important to point out that animal communicators aren't infallible. They're human and they make mistakes. "This is not science; it is an interaction," says Ginny Debbink.

I urge you to approach an animal communication session with an open mind and enough faith in the communicator that you don't have to hold back information in order to "test" the communicator before you can take stock in what she has to say. Provide her with enough information to have a productive discussion with your animal. If you need proof, it will doubtless come.

A TYPICAL ANIMAL COMMUNICATION SESSION

Not all animal communicators operate the same way. But there are common threads that run through most sessions with animal communicators. A typical communication session takes place with the client on the phone with the communicator. An appointment is made in advance, in many cases, and the client calls the communicator at the appointed time. The communicator will ask the client for some basic information about the animal so that she is sure to contact the right animal. That basic information usually includes name, species, type (such as breed or mix), gender, and perhaps the animal's coloring. Some communicators request a photo of the animal before the session, so that they can create a mental image of the animal they're contacting.

As mysterious as it sounds, it's not difficult for the communicator to make a connection with the right animal. She uses your energy and the love you feel for your animal to help her connect. As you describe your animal to the communicator, your animal tunes in. "It's just like getting the right telephone number or radio station," says Penelope Smith, who acknowledges that just talking about it intellectually makes it sound "kind of weird." But it happens so often and easily that it's not remarkable to her. "It really is as easy as dialing a telephone," she says.

You have to expect a lot of silence during a communication session over the phone. At the beginning, there will be silence as the communicator makes the connection with the animal. In most cases, the communicator will ask permission of the animal to have the conversation (a negative answer is rare). Once the connection has been made and your animal has given permission to talk, you ask your first question.

There's silence as the communicator relays the question telepathically to your animal. (It can be hard to sit still and listen to dead air, but you must try to put your mind at peace and focus on your animal.) Then there's more silence as your animal sends his response back to the communicator. After a bit, you'll hear what your animal friend has to say.

And what is the animal doing during the communication session? You might expect him to be alert, wondering where this "voice" is coming from. You might even think your animal would look startled. But typically, that's not the way it goes. Animals communicate telepathically all of the time, so surprise doesn't really factor into the equation. They're used to receiving our communication. In a structured session, the difference is that there's a human who is receiving his telepathic messages and actually responding to them.

In all the sessions I've had with Kramer and Scout, they've relaxed, even slept, during the session, usually staying in the same room with me. I've learned that this isn't unusual.

"Normally animals get very relaxed in a session because it is so pleasurable for them," communicator Gail De Sciose told me before her session with Kramer and Scout. "They have been listening to us and now it is their turn to talk and have us listen to them."

When Joan Brosia has Gail speak with her family of birds—19 in all, both domestic and wild species—the normally chattering birds became absolutely still the moment the communication begins. As soon as she hangs up the phone, the house comes alive and the rooms are filled with the sound of chattering. "They always have a big discussion afterwards," says Joan.

Sometimes an animal will do something to let you know he's feeling connected with you during a session. When Janyne Kizer spoke with her Lab, Penny, through Ginny Debbink, Penny surprised Janyne by going upstairs and sitting next to her during the session. "She normally stays downstairs until bedtime," says Janyne.

Similarly, when Cathy Barash spoke with her cat Tiarella through Gail De Sciose, the kitty lay down on her side on the dining room table right in front of Cathy throughout the session. It was a highly unusual place for her to lie down and an unusual position for her to lie in. When Cathy finished talking with Tiarella and turned the conversation to Sebastian, Cathy's departed cat, Tiarella hopped off the table and left the room, as if to afford her some privacy.

During the client's conversation with her animal friend, the animal communicator acts as an interpreter. More than likely, she's not giving a verbatim transcript of what the animal has said, since animals use all their senses to communicate. The communicator may have heard words, or she may have felt emotions or physical sensations. She may have seen images or even smelled odors. It's up to her to put all those sensory messages into words that she can relay to the client. This is a special skill in and of itself.

Ginny Debbink says that all the information comes to her through so many different channels simultaneously that she often can't identify them individually. She describes the information she gets from the animal simply as a "knowing" that she then translates to the client.

Animals are individuals and, just as some humans are more communicative than others, so are some animals. Animals who live closely with humans tend to develop our use of language. Sometimes an animal communicator will be able to actually quote her client's animal friend, which is a fun way to gain insight into the animal's personality. My poodle, Scout, is a dog who knows what she wants. Once, she requested through Ginny Debbink that her dad rub her belly more often. I protested that my husband does rub her belly. Her simple response spoke volumes about her considerable self-esteem: "He should do nothing else."

The communicator's conversation with the client's animal continues in this way, with the client supplying questions or responses to the communicator who in turn relays them to the animal and back again.

The Simplicity of a Session

When he experienced his first animal communication session with his Chesapeake Bay Retriever, Quaid, Michael McCarthy was struck by the ease with which Gail De Sciose was able to obtain answers to all his questions. Quaid is a happy, relatively uncomplicated dog, but Michael somehow expected the process to be more complex. For each question he asked, there was a simple answer that made perfect sense. "I wasn't ready for the simplicity of it," Michael said. "I've been through psychoanalysis myself and there always has to be a reason for everything."

For example, Michael was concerned that Quaid tended to hoard his toys and carry them around with him. Michael feared that his attachment to his toys would lead to possessive aggression down the road (never mind that Quaid always happily gives his toy up to anyone who asks; he just grabs another). So Michael asked Quaid about it. The answer was simple. Quaid likes the feeling of having something in his mouth. "I had blown this up into a pet behavior nightmare," says Michael. "It is such a simple answer, but I couldn't find it on my own."

PREPARING FOR THE CONVERSATION

Communicators generally charge by the duration of the session. The client will schedule a 30-minute session, for example, and the conversation ends at the end of that half hour. A half-hour is a fairly typical length for a session, though some communicators offer sessions that last for as few as 15 minutes; for others an hour might be the rule.

In order to make the most of the time a client has with the communicator (which, in my experience, goes by very quickly, no matter how much time is allotted), it's a good idea to prepare some questions in advance, and prioritize them. The client should leave some time at the end of the conversation (or take time at the beginning) to ask if her animals have anything they want to tell her. She might be surprised at what they have to say.

By posing this last question in a session, I learned that Kramer does not want any more dogs to be part of our family. I hadn't been considering adding any animals and so had never asked his opinion about it (though I certainly would have before bringing in another animal). But he told me, unsolicited and in no uncertain terms, that two animals for two humans was just the right ratio.

Sharon Callahan encourages her clients to have questions prepared before their session, but she prefers to start the session by asking the animal what he'd like to talk about. "I simply allow the animal to speak and address the issues that are important to him," she says. "So often the issue at hand is not what the person expects." Sharon says that most of the client's questions are addressed naturally at some point during the conversation, but it's a good idea to have them written down to make sure they're covered.

Not all communicators set up appointments. Lydia Hiby does consultations two days a week. On her consultation days, she sits by the phone and talks with whoever gets through. She found that making appointments, only to have clients forget or cancel them, frustrating. So she lets fate decide who she will be speaking with. "Usually the people who really need to get to me get through to me," she says.

Other communicators prefer to speak with the animals without the client on the line. Alice McClure, for example, does a pre-interview, of sorts, with the animal. When a client calls for a consultation, she takes down the information about the animal and what the person is hoping to learn from him. She'll set up an appointment for the client to call back for the session and in the intervening time period she will take some quiet time and have a conversation with the animal to get the ball rolling. "I feel the preparation helps me direct the flow better [during the phone consult]," she says.

The Frightened Caller

Many people approach an initial animal communication session with a certain amount of trepidation. "I get a lot of people who are breathtakingly nervous," says Ginny Debbink. "They are so nervous they can't even speak." Usually, she says, the nervousness dissipates within the first five minutes of the session.

What are they afraid of? Dawn Hayman says that they tend to be afraid of what their animal might say. What if the animal tells on them for some perceived infraction? Or, worse, what if the animal says they don't love their human?

This rarely happens, says Dawn. "I've never talked to an animal who hated the human," she says. "Animals aren't judgmental; they are very forgiving." Of course, an animal communicator's clients are a self-selected group. If they didn't have strong relationships with their animal friends, they probably wouldn't be paying someone to converse with them.

Sharing your animal's thoughts and emotions with a perfect stranger (before you even get a chance to hear those thoughts yourself) is understandably daunting. It's not unlike spilling your soul to a marriage counselor. But professional animal communicators don't sit in judgment. "I think it is such intimate time and I respect that," says Lydia Hiby.

A good animal communicator is a conduit for the communication between the client and her animal friend. While she may provide advice, encouragement or suggestions for solutions to problems, she shouldn't be intrusive. If you use the services of a professional animal communicator, you may end up feeling like clients I interviewed, all of whom universally praised the animal communicator with whom they worked.

One example is the particularly well-stated praise that client Helen Koster offered up for Gail De Sciose: "Gail's intentions are so high," she told me. "In a world of specialization, where an analytical mind is so valued, Gail is like a throwback, like the general practitioner of years gone by. She has that incredible willingness. She doesn't look for drama. She is clean and pure and well-intentioned."

Chapter 3

Are Communicators for Real?

··

Americans are always wary about being ripped off. Our fraud radar is very sensitive: We're always on the look out for someone trying to take our money. Thanks to the proliferation of psychic hot lines that you can call for a fee, many people greet the idea of telepathic animal communication with skepticism. Initially, I too had strong doubts.

The pragmatists among us point out that there is no scientific evidence that telepathic animal communication exists. "Because they don't have visual proof, people don't want to buy it," says Ginny Debbink. But many people who use the services of an animal communicator receive proof when the communicator tells them things that they couldn't possibly know unless it came from the animal. Sure, that sort of evidence is "only" anecdotal (a dirty word among the scientific set), but when it's your anecdote, it's mighty powerful.

I spoke to a number of people who had many such experiences. Even if they were skeptical at the outset, that skepticism was put to rest in fairly short order. How? In some cases, the animal communicator innocently passed on a mind-blowing revelation. In others, the client received instant results after a communication. Either way, the communicator quickly made believers out of the following people.

The first time that Catherine Mills met animal communicator Patty Summers (with whom she would have a long relationship), she brought along three of her dogs. One of them, Solar, was two weeks pregnant, not far enough along for her pregnancy to be apparent. Patty got down on the floor with the dogs, and Solar crawled into her lap. Patty squealed, "She's going to have five puppies!" Roughly six weeks later, Solar gave birth to five puppies.

Roni Bailey of South Salem, N.Y., has eight cats, two dogs, a duck and a ferret. When animal communicator Gail De Sciose was speaking with Roni's dog, Murphy, she asked (on Roni's behalf), who Murphy's favorite animal companion was. Murphy hemmed and hawed a little and said, "This is going to sound strange to you…it's a duck." Gail had no way of knowing that Roni had a duck. But, according to Murphy, the duck and Murphy speak together all the time about an important topic they have in common: Their love for Roni and "how she saved their hearts."

During a communication session with Ginny Debbink, Gina Barnett asked her dog, Fred, what was important to him (since he'd just informed her that, long or short, toenails aren't important). He replied, "You, patience, kindness, and…" Ginny started to stumble a little over what Fred said next. "Toe, tofu? Something like tofu, but that's not quite it," she said. Gina asked, "Tapu?" "Yes," said Ginny, "that's it." Tapu is a dear friend of Gina's. Fred told Ginny that he loves Tapu's soft energy. "Tapu is a lovely, grounded, spiritual person who loves all animals, and Fred obviously adores her!" says Gina.

Sometimes our animals might provide little tidbits that can be slightly embarrassing. Abby Jaye has two dogs, Scooby and Ginger. One day they related a fact to Lydia Hiby that Lydia could not have known. The dogs told Lydia something personal (and true): Abby walks around the house in the nude.

The first time that Lydia spoke with Scooby, the mixed-breed dog told her that he was upset because a man at a nursing home had teased him about being neutered. When Lydia related this to Abby, she confirmed that on a pet-therapy visit the previous day, a senior citizen had teasingly asked Scooby, who was lying on his back as part of a trick, "What's the matter, you ain't got no balls?" Abby hadn't realized that this had bothered Scooby so much, but it was foremost on his mind.

Touché, Michele Hegedus' cat, one day told Gail De Sciose that he was really concerned because Michele had been crying. "I had been going through some personal problems, and holding them inside of me until I came home," says Michele. And, yes, she'd been crying.

Stacey Vornbrock is an old friend of Sonya Fitzpatrick—she knew her even before Sonya rediscovered her childhood ability to communicate with animals. Stacey's animals were among the first animals with whom Sonya practiced animal communication. Stacey never doubted Sonya's abilities. If she had, though, any doubts would have vanished. "She said things that were so dead on accurate that there was no way she could have known," says Stacey. For example, her cats will tell Sonya that Stacey has a new haircut or new clothes (and they'll offer their opinion about it). Invariably, if the cats mentioned something new to Sonya, something new had occurred.

Susan Kalev was injured one night when her cat, Soho, who is deaf, jumped up from his spot at the foot of her bed and ran across her, obviously spooked. In the process, he dug his claws deeply into Susan's arm.

Susan couldn't imagine what had frightened her cat so. She asked Gail De Sciose to ask him. Gail said that Soho told her there was some kind of light that had come into the dark room suddenly from the outside and he needed to get away from it.

Susan remembered that just before Soho started his frantic scramble across her, a truck passed by their apartment and light streamed into the window. Susan could hear the coming truck, and so she wasn't alarmed by the light. But being deaf, Soho was frightened by the sudden, inexplicable light. "To me, that was absolute proof that Gail was communicating with my animals," says Susan.

Mary Kay Keppler, who lives in the desert near Phoenix, was horrified when her husband came running in from the garage one evening saying, "Where are the dogs?" He'd heard the loud and unmistakable sound of a rattlesnake's rattle and saw a coiled rattler in their yard, outside the dog run.

They ran to the door and saw their 7.5-pound Yorkshire Terrier, Callie, standing not four feet away from the rattler, stiff as a board, slowly moving her tail. "She was poised and ready to attack if need be," remembers Mary Kay.

Thankfully, there was a gate between the two, enough to keep Callie from attacking the snake, though the snake could certainly have come under the gate and bitten the little dog.

Mary Kay scooped Callie up and brought her in the house to safety.

Mary Kay, a regular client of Ginny Debbink's, wanted to know what was going through Callie's mind as she faced off the rattlesnake. She didn't give Ginny any background information, just told her that they'd had a little incident in the yard, and asked whether Callie had been scared.

Callie told Ginny that she'd been aroused and that if the gate had not been there she would have gotten closer. Did she think she had to kill it? Yes. Callie called her foe "a dangerous monster ground-dweller that smells like spices and the earth." (I spoke with Bob Myers, director of the American International Rattlesnake Museum in Albuquerque, who told me that rattlesnakes do emit a smell, though he would characterize it as sweet, not spicy.)

Callie added that Mary Kay shouldn't worry because Callie would give up her life before she would let the monster get Mary Kay. (Somehow I don't think that allayed Mary Kay's worries.)

After she'd related that information, Ginny asked, "What was it, a snake?"

Michele Hegedus' cat, Touché, enjoyed scratching his neck and chin on the shade of the lamp on Michele's bedside table. The lamp itself was brass and tended to heat up a bit when the light was on. Since the tabletop was polished wood, Michele feared that if Touché became startled, he might slide on the slick surface and make contact with the lamp, possibly burning himself in the process. She was prepared to simply dispose of the lamp, but decided to ask Gail De Sciose to explain to Touché why his practice was dangerous.

Gail started out by asking Touché why he loved rubbing against the lampshade so much. He explained that its woven linen surface did a particularly nice job of scratching his neck. Gail told him why Michele didn't want him to rub on the lampshade. Michele offered to buy special brushes and pay special attention to scratching his neck if he would stop scratching it on the lamp.

That night, after the conversation, Touché came into the bedroom as usual, jumped up on the bed and headed for the lamp, like he did every night. But this night, he stopped at the edge of the bed, rather than jumping onto the bedside table. He sat down and stared at the lamp with a cocked head. Then he looked right at Michele, making eye contact with her, then looked back at the lamp. He then jumped up, went to the end of the bed, curled up and went to sleep.

"He never touched the lamp again, and he never even attempted to rub against it," says Michele. She did her part by buying special brushes for him and even installed a corner brush, which affixes to the wall at cat-neck height, so that he could brush himself whenever he wanted.

The first time that Dorothy Fogle had a session with Sonya Fitzpatrick, any skepticism she had vanished. "She told me things that were unbelievable," remembers Dorothy. For instance, Dorothy had been planning a trip, and Jacob, her Conure, heard her making plane reservations. The bird asked Sonya to ask Dorothy who would be taking care of him while she was gone. He asked, "Is it going to be the fat lady who has her hair hanging in her face?" Dorothy was amazed, because the woman who usually took care of him fit that description exactly. "There was no way in the world that Sonya would know about that except from Jacob," she says.

Helen Koster's cat, Lillian, was extremely fearful her entire life. When Lillian was suffering from diarrhea, Helen didn't want to take her to the veterinarian because the trip out of the apartment was so traumatic for Lillian. First, she decided, she would call Gail De Sciose and see if she could help her identify the problem and see if it might be easily remedied.

This was the first time that Helen had consulted with Gail. As it happened, Helen lived across the street from Gail in New York City, so Gail offered to make a house call.

Fully aware that Lillian might not greet her at all, Gail asked if she could meditate in the bedroom in which Lillian was hiding. Gail meditated quietly for about ten minutes. At the end of the meditation, she communicated telepathically with Lillian, explaining that Helen had asked Gail to come over to talk with her. Gail told Lillian that she would truly like to see her and asked whether she might consider coming out of hiding so that Gail could see what she looked like. Gail promised not to touch her. "She came out from behind her chair and sat by my knee and looked at me," says Gail. "It was a first for Lillian."

Gail then said to Lillian, "I know you have a friend named Annie." Lillian must have then said something telepathically to Annie, Helen's other cat, because at that moment Annie jumped out of Helen's arms and came to the door. "Lillian met Annie at the door to introduce her to Gail," remembers Helen.

Gail was able to help Lillian with her diarrhea. When she connected with Lillian, Gail felt incredible gas in her own body. She suggested to Helen that a change of diet might help. And it did.

Helen's other cat, Annie, is quite the opposite of her friend Lillian: She likes to be included in everything. Helen and her husband take Annie with them in the car. One day, they drove with Annie up to a scenic area and turned around and drove back without getting out of the car. The next time that Helen had a consultation with Gail, she said to Gail, "We took Annie on a trip." When Gail related that to Annie, her retort was, "They didn't take me on a trip. They took me on a ride. A trip is when you get out of the car." Of course, Gail had no idea that they hadn't gotten out of the car.

These stories are not fabrications. Make an appointment with a communicator and see for yourself.

Chapter 4

Strengthening Your Relationship with Your Animal

....

Before I discovered animal communication, I was constantly wishing I knew what my Standard Poodles Kramer and Scout were thinking. It felt like I was searching for the Holy Grail. If I could somehow know exactly what was going through their minds, I would have the key to their happiness.

That wasn't particularly realistic. When I finally was able to talk with my dogs (through Ginny Debbink), all our problems didn't magically disappear; but I sure did feel closer to my dogs—and they to me, I believe. Once you've had a two-way conversation with your animals and learned what they feel and what's important to them, it changes your perspective forever. You can't help but view your animal friends as more complete beings, with opinions, feelings and reasons for their actions.

Those reasons might be innate to their species—something that's important to bear in mind. Even when your animal friends can communicate their motivations to you, those motivations might not make a lot of sense to you as a human. But you should respect their motivations and recognize that, as similar as we are in terms of emotions, humans and animals have hard-wired differences.

I was close to my dogs before animal communication. I loved them completely. But I didn't have a complete understanding of who they were as individuals. I learned things about them—especially about Scout—that made perfect sense but that I was oblivious to until Ginny Debbink communicated with them.

For example, Scout has extremely high self-esteem and looks down her nose at other dogs who are ugly in her eyes. The less like a Poodle a dog looks, the less attractive (and therefore less worthy) they are. I guess some might call her a snob. This plays out over and over as she "shouts" (as she calls it) at dogs with snub noses or especially short legs. I may not be happy that she tends to be haughty around Basset Hounds, but at least I now understand where that behavior is coming from.

COMMUNICATION—BRINGING PEOPLE AND ANIMALS CLOSER TOGETHER

Whenever I finish an animal communication session with my dogs, I feel enveloped by love for them. There's nothing like a good talk to make you feel close to someone. I think the feeling is mutual.

Imagine what a thrill it must be for the animal to actually have his person listening to what he has to say. "When you meet someone new and you have a conversation with them and they really want to know about you, you feel closer to them," says Robert Mueller, D.V.M., a veterinarian (and Kramer and Scout's chiropractor) and husband of animal communicator Nancy Mueller. "An animal communication session can work the same way to make an animal and person closer."

One of Nancy Mueller's clients, Diane Beuthe, says that talking with her animals through Nancy definitely helps her relationship with them. Diane has horses, dogs, cats, chickens, and a canary. "Animal communication has given me a total understanding of them," she says.

"I can openly communicate with them about injuries, mood swings, reasons why they are behaving the way they are. I can also reassure them."

Susan Rifkin Ajamian is a client and close friend of Anita Curtis. She asks Anita to talk with her horses and cats frequently. Her world opened up when she became exposed to animal communication, she says. "Animal communication has enhanced my relationship with animals in general and with my companions in particular because it confirmed my wish and belief that animals understand us; that when we talk with them we are carrying on a conversation with a sentient, often wise and loving individual."

One of Lydia Hiby's clients, Carol Albino, talks with her horses and dogs through Lydia. "I think I respect their intelligence more than I ever did," she says. "It makes them so easy to deal with. When I think about them in a different light and give them a little more credit, it saves a lot of heartache."

Amy Nowak, who uses Dawn Hayman's services every six weeks to talk with the horses she works with, says about animal communication, "I love it. It is something I do for myself."

Amy doesn't always have major issues to address when she talks with her horses. "I check to make sure that they are comfortable. Saddle fit is very important." When Amy re-shoes a horse or introduces some new equipment, she'll talk with the horse through Dawn to make sure everything's okay.

But for Amy, animal communication is more than checking on the horses and making sure life's good. It provides real benefits in terms of her relationship with her animals. "I am a lot more connected now," she says. "The relationship blossoms and animal communication gives it more depth." When she talks with her animals, she says, her heart opens up and she appreciates them so much more. "It's wonderful to appreciate what incredible souls they are and what gifts they give me."

An animal communication session can help you identify discord in your own life that your animal recognizes and, perhaps, is reacting to.

"Most of my communications involve showing the person something, from the animal's perspective, that is off in his or her life," says Sharon Callahan. Sharon says that during a session she is more often than not reading a person's life situation from the animal's point of view. An animal communication session certainly is not just about the animal.

Michele Hegedus, a client of Gail De Sciose, agrees. Michele says that animal communication has helped her understand her place in the universe. "Once you have a communication with your animal, you never look at animals the same way again," she says. "It's impossible to."

That change in perspective is a very rewarding aspect of an animal communicator's work. "The subtle shift in the way people view their animals after a consultation keeps me doing the work," Ginny Debbink says. "Even those in a relationship with their pets view them as less of a possession after a session."

Patty Summers agrees, "I really like helping people to understand the animal's perspective and see things from a different place. From understanding comes harmony."

Michele Hegedus consulted Gail before bringing a special cat into her life. Cassis was turned over to the ASPCA after she was found abandoned in the street. The young gray and beige cat had no eyeballs. She had eye sockets and lashes, but, of course, was completely blind. Veterinarians at the ASPCA assumed that she was born with the condition. Because she was getting infections in the eye socket, due to inward-growing eyelashes, veterinarians removed Cassie's eyelashes and sutured her eyes shut.

At the time, Michele worked at the ASPCA and fell in love with the cat. After Cassis was well enough to be adopted (she was in bad shape when she was brought in on Christmas Eve), Michele took her home. But first, she asked Gail to talk with not only Cassis, but with Touché, her other cat. Gail told Touché about Cassis and her special needs and asked whether he would welcome her into the family. He said he understood her needs and that he would help with her.

He was as good as his word. Touché takes very good care of Cassis, grooming her after she eats, and making sure she is eating before he begins his own meal. The two cats rest and play together.

Animal communication can help not only your relationship with your animal companion, but also your animals' relationships with one another. Gail has played a big role in helping Touché and Cassis build their relationship. Eye contact and body language are important parts of a cat's communication repertoire, and since Cassis is blind, Touché's posturing is lost on her. Cassis doesn't posture at all, says Michele. So Gail fills the void. She explained to Cassis that sometimes Touché needs a rest from her relentless playing. She showed Cassis a mental image of the perch upon which Touché takes sanctuary from Cassis and explained that when he's there, he needs a rest and she should leave him alone. Cassis understands and respects that.

Sometimes Touché will resort to body language that Cassis doesn't have to have eyes to understand. If she's bugging him and he's had enough, he will sit down in front of her and bop her on the head with his paw.

"Cassis has been very good for Touché," says Michele. Touché, once a terrified shelter cat, is now more exuberant, curious and happy. Michele says that when she comes home from work, she sees the two cats sitting in the window, waiting for her. Touché sits and looks out the window. Cassis always sits facing Touché. "It's as if she is getting impressions and feedback from him about what he's seeing," says Michele.

Gail spoke with Cassis before Michele brought her home from the shelter. She telepathically sent Cassis images of Michele's home (which Gail had visited) and of toys and other cat paraphernalia, to help her acclimate easily. When she sent Cassis an image of Michele, Cassis commented, "She is so pretty."

Cassis has never let her blindness slow her down. She lives life with great enthusiasm. She races through her apartment, bumping into things only occasionally. Michele conscientiously has cat-proofed the entire apartment (to the point where she removes the light bulbs from the floor lamps before leaving the house for fear that Cassis will succeed in climbing a lamp and knocking it over). She doesn't rearrange furniture without taking Cassis around in her arms and showing her where everything is. And she makes sure that objects aren't placed in Cassis' path. "It's like having a two-year-old in the house," says Michele.

Michele fears that Cassis will injure herself with the reckless abandon with which she lives life. She's asked Gail to talk with her about it. Cassis doesn't share that fear. "Nothing can happen to me because Michele takes such good care of me," she says.

Zara Heartwood took in a six-month-old Shetland Sheepdog puppy, whom she named Rainbow, shortly before her beloved Golden Retriever, Sunny, died suddenly of cancer. Rainbow was a frightened dog who had never been outside of his dog run.

Seven months after Sunny's death, Zara found herself resenting Rainbow, who was a high-needs dog due to his fearfulness and separation anxiety. "I hated Rainbow for being alive while Sunny was dead," she says.

She took Rainbow to see an animal communicator, Elaine Thompson, to see if she could help with the Sheltie's separation anxiety. Elaine talked with Rainbow and told Zara that Rainbow was freaked out because Zara was so mad at her all the time. Rainbow said, "I don't know where I fit in and I don't feel secure. I feel you are going to leave me."

"I was in such grief over Sunny," Zara remembers, "and it wasn't Rainbow's fault." Zara made a commitment to keep Rainbow.

A year later, after having adopted three more needy dogs, Zara had another conversation with her animals through Elaine. Rainbow told Elaine proudly, "I am the queen. I am the alpha. My mom loves me best."

"What a contrast from a year ago!" says Zara, who thinks that Rainbow's confidence started to increase after the initial session with Elaine. Knowing Rainbow's perspective really helped Zara to not be angry with her, she says. "Knowing that, like me, she missed Sunny helped a lot too."

A ROSE BY ANY OTHER NAME

An animal's name is very important. Some names are self-fulfilling, says Dawn Hayman. Names such as "Killer" and "Devil's Revenge" can have an impact on how others view an animal and how he views himself. "Your dog will live up to his name," says Dawn. It's particularly important not to give these names to Dobermans or Rottweilers, she says. "Dobies and Rotties are very sensitive. They sense when people are afraid or cross the street to avoid them and it is hard for them. They don't understand."

Abby Jaye learned that she had unwittingly made it difficult for her dog to behave by naming her Scrappy. Abby already had another dog named Scooby, so she named her new dog Scrappy, in keeping with the cartoon theme. Scrappy turned out to be aggressive with other dogs. A year after she'd named her dog Scrappy, she learned from Lydia Hiby that Scrappy meant "fighter." At Lydia's suggestion (actually, at her insistence), Scrappy was renamed. After a good deal of deliberation, Abby and her husband selected the name Ginger, which means "animated." "The name change really helped," says Abby. "She became a lot less aggressive."

A name can have an effect on an animal's self-esteem. When Mickey Merriam adopted a Papillon who had been a puppy mill brood bitch, she shuddered at the dog's unfortunate name: Pattycakes. She loathed the name so much she couldn't bear to use it, so she shortened it to PK (the little dog didn't respond to PC).

When she spoke with PK through Ginny Debbink, she asked how PK felt about her name. "Anything is better than Pattycakes," the Papillon told her, "but PK is just initials." She said she'd like a real name.

Mickey decided to rename her Patricia, which she felt was a strong, intelligent name. Patricia responded immediately. In a subsequent conversation with Ginny, Patricia told Mickey that she loves her name and that she thinks it is beautiful.

Cheryl Weeks consulted Dawn Hayman when she was trying to find a name for her Australian Shepherd puppy. She tried for weeks to come up with a name for him. Cheryl can frequently communicate telepathically with her own animals, so she tried talking with him about his name. "Since he was a young pup, I couldn't get any clear answers from him," she recalls. "The only thing that kept coming through was Will or Wills or Willis, but I wasn't sure."

When she called Dawn, the puppy made Dawn laugh. He said that Cheryl was close on his name, that she could call him Will or Wills if she wanted to, but she must not call him Willie or Billy. He hated those names. "Truthfully" he said (in a very stuffy tone), "My name is William." Cheryl was not inclined to argue. "He might come to you if you call him Will or Wills," says Cheryl, "but he will immediately look at you or come to you if you call him William!"

Some animals feel they have a true name (though most don't insist that they be called it). My own dog, Scout, for example, came to us as a three-year-old with the name Trixie. We felt she deserved a more dignified name, so we gave her the name of the spunky little girl protagonist of a favorite novel, *To Kill a Mockingbird*. Two years later, in our first animal communication session with Ginny Debbink, Scout told me that her real, true name is "Freesia." I had no idea. But Scout said she didn't mind the name we'd given her, so we decided to stick with Scout.

Gina Barnett had a dream in which Fred, her Great Dane/Lab mix told her that his real name is "Mighty Kitchen." "When I woke up I had to admit that Mighty Kitchen was a name that Fred would likely come up with," says Gina. When she had a communication with Ginny Debbink, she asked Fred about the name. Fred laughed and said that she had to look at it from a dog's point of view. The kitchen is the most important room in the house, and he is the mightiest. "It's a name which conveys both space and function," Fred told Gina. Gina enjoys calling Fred by his new nickname on occasion.

ANIMALS AS TEACHERS

In the course of researching this book, I repeatedly heard from clients of animal communicators how their animals were their teachers. "She has taught me so much" and "I don't know how I'd live without him" were constant refrains.

Patti Limber rescues homeless ferrets and is devoted to her charges. When one special ferret, Shadow, became ill, Patti sought the services of an animal communicator, who in turn introduced her to alternative healing modalities like Reiki, flower essences and others. "All of these things were Shadow's lessons; these lessons have truly changed my life and how I assist the animals entrusted in my care." Shadow passed away after more than five years with Patti. "The depth of my relationship with Shadow will live in my heart forever," she says.

For Mickey Merriam, who adopted Patricia, the abused Papillon, she has learned an important virtue: patience. The frightened little dog still won't let Mickey touch her, after an entire year in her new home. But thanks to Ginny, Mickey knows that Patricia is happy in her home and Mickey is satisfied with the incremental progress that Patricia is making. Patricia feels badly, she told Ginny, that she can't ask Mickey to hold her or pick her up, but she says she feels more loved. Mickey knows the patience that Patricia has taught her is paying off.

Gina Barnett's Fred told her through Ginny that he is here to teach people a lightness of being, to bring a clearer perspective on not taking things too seriously. "The greatest prophets were also good laughers," he said. Gina is committed to learning that lesson. "Part of my journey is to learn this lightness from him," she says.

Katherine Roberts' life revolves around her animals, but that wasn't always the case. She credits her Rocky Mountain horse, Chauncey, with the wonderful direction her life has taken. Katherine raises Icelandic horses on a farm in western Massachusetts that was once her weekend home. As caring for her animals (dogs and cats in addition to the horses) took up more and more of her time, she decided to devote herself to the animals.

Despite her devotion, she was for a number of years ambivalent about keeping Chauncey, since she'd turned her attention to Icelandic horses. She would speak to friends from time to time about selling Chauncey.

When Chauncey attacked a new Icelandic horse, Katherine bowed to her husband's wishes to sell Chauncey. But she couldn't bear to have him far away, so she offered him to a neighbor as a gift. "My heart was broken, but at the time I couldn't see a way around it."

A mere week later, Helen glanced out her window and saw Chauncey walking up the driveway. He had jumped the fence and come home.

At that point, Katherine told Chauncey that he had a home with her for the rest of his life. "I had to go through this to realize what a bond I had with him," she says. "I just couldn't take our relationship so lightly."

Katherine, who speaks with her animals through Gail De Sciose, is grateful to Chauncey for giving her another chance. "He was giving me the space to find out what I had to learn about my relationship with animals," she says.

DEEP THOUGHTS

With the help of telepathic communication, you might learn that your animal is very deep. Maybe you suspected this, or maybe it comes as a shock. Some of the people I interviewed shared some very deep thoughts from their animal friends, who are obviously wise souls.

For example, Sherry Moore's dog, Dudley, a Lab/Dalmatian mix who was rescued from the road after being hit by a car and left to die, shared some important sentiments with Sherry when she spoke with him through Patty Summers. He said, "Harmony is my energy, my gift I bring. I belong here because I bring balance, softness to the one who craves it [Sherry's sometimes-grumbly Doberman, Niko], and to the one who needs it [her fearful Dobie, Kellie]."

Dudley went on to say to Sherry, "I look deep into your eyes and they are filled with love. I feel your warmth and often bask in it. It feels like the sun penetrating my soul."

And to Sharon's husband, Artie, Dudley had this to say: "I look into your heart and feel such softness, tenderness and I am reminded of myself. You are an honorable man who struggles with your human world. Be in nature, allow your real self to come out more."

Would that we could all receive—and heed—such sage advice from our animal friends.

Chapter 5

Learn Your Companion Animal's History

··

Adopting an adult animal can be a very rewarding experience. Providing a good home to an animal who needs it is a wonderful thing, particularly if the animal is otherwise facing euthanasia. The downside to adopting an adult animal—or any age animal that you don't take directly from his mother—is that you're unaware of his experiences before he joined your life. Those experiences can have had a great influence on the development of his personality. For example, a particular trauma of which you are unaware may be the cause of certain behavioral idiosyncrasies.

Being able to learn about your animal friend's prior experiences might provide a clue in helping you understand and modify his behavior. Or you might simply just be curious about why your animal acts the way he does. Animal communication can help you unlock the mysteries of your animal's past.

That is, if your animal's willing to talk about it. My own dog, Scout, was adopted at the age of three. Naturally, I was curious about what went on in her life before we got her. I had some ideas, since I knew she'd been out loose, hit by a car, and her owners took her to the vet to be euthanized. (The good-hearted vet instead patched up her broken leg and found her a new home with us.) But when I asked Scout about her former family in our first conversation through Ginny Debbink, she didn't want to talk about it. She told me what I'd already assumed, that her old family didn't give her the respect that we did ("They treated me like a dog," she complained), but beyond that she said no more except that they hadn't been cruel to her. I had hoped to learn more, but because the information wasn't vital, I certainly didn't press the point.

The information about Scout's prior life wasn't that important to me, since we weren't trying to get to the root of any behavioral issues. But for others, being able to tap into that information has not only increased their understanding of their animals, but has also given them the chance to ensure that history won't be repeated. And that can go a long way toward healing old wounds and changing undesirable behavior.

Carol Albino, a client of Lydia Hiby, had a Border Collie named Floss who was six years old when she came to live with the Albino family. For a full four months, Floss wouldn't even acknowledge the existence of Carol's husband. Not only did she not look at him, she completely ignored him.

With Lydia's help, they found out that the dog had been trained, by a man, through the extensive use of a shock collar. The result was a deep-seated fear of men. Through Lydia, Carol's husband and her dog had a long talk, in which the husband reassured Floss that he would never, ever use such tactics on her. From that point on, their relationship improved greatly and they're good friends now.

Carol is in a position to place a lot of dogs in need of homes because people tend to drop dogs off near her ranch. Carol always hires Lydia to talk with the dogs about their history to help Carol place them in appropriate homes. One of these dogs, an Australian Shepherd named Susie, told Lydia that she had been given up because she enjoyed digging so much. Carol decided to keep Susie and learned firsthand the accuracy of these conversations. Susie loves nothing more than to dig. But thanks to Lydia, at least Carol knew what she was getting herself into!

When Sherry Moore took in Kasey, a seven-year-old Doberman Pinscher, she was dismayed that Kasey chose to bite Sherry's other four dogs during her first week in the Moore home. Sherry asked Patty Summers to ask Kasey why she was biting. It was obvious she had something to prove. "I'm stronger than they are," she said. Kasey admitted that her former person had encouraged her to bite. She expected Sherry to approve of her biting as well, and was surprised that instead of praise she was put in a crate each time she'd bitten.

Sherry, through Patty, explained that if Kasey didn't get past her affinity for biting the other dogs, they'd have to find her a new home. Kasey said she would be willing to try. The biting soon subsided, and only continued when Kasey was faced with certain triggers, such as toys, that Sherry can fortunately control.

Mickey Merriam adopted Patricia the Papillon to keep her other Pap, Bandit, company. She was especially thrilled to give Patricia a good home, since the little dog had spent her first three years in the hell of a puppy mill, where she was a brood bitch who had litter after litter until she was given up because the puppy mill owner didn't like the quality of her puppies.

Growing up in that environment, Patricia was afraid of her own shadow. Even a year after being in a loving home, she still cannot abide being petted by Mickey, though she is slowly getting more comfortable in her new home.

Mickey was disappointed that Patricia couldn't accept her love. She contacted Ginny Debbink in order to talk with Patricia and see if she could figure out how to help her more. "I had Ginny work with her because even after six months I couldn't touch her," says Mickey. Patricia told Ginny that she was abused so badly in the puppy mill, and had given her trust to so many people who had let her down, that she just couldn't trust anymore.

This knowledge gave Mickey the patience to keep working with Patricia to gain her trust. "She's coming along," she acknowledges.

Ginny also helped Mickey solve another mystery: Why Patricia refused to come through the door into the house from the backyard when Mickey would hold the screen door open for her. As long as Mickey stood there, Patricia refused to walk in. Ginny found out that at the puppy mill, a person would hold a door open for her, then put her foot up to stop Patricia when she tried to go by. (An adult person's foot at eye level of a Papillon is bound to be a scary thing.) Patricia couldn't trust that Mickey wouldn't do this.

At Ginny's suggestion, Mickey began simply to go through the door and hold it open from behind the screen door. "There are times when I can see in her eyes that she doesn't know what I'm going to do. But most of the time she will go ahead and come in."

Tania Smothers adopted a Dobie mix, whom she named Merlin, from a shelter. The staff at the shelter had named the dog Racer because of the "racing stripe" down his back—a scar that ran down his spine from the base of his neck to the base of his tail. The shelter veterinarian told her that Merlin had been abused and that the vet had had to amputate his tail, but gave no more details.

Tania contacted Patty Summers to try to gain some insight into what had happened to Merlin. She wanted to know how he had received that scar, which resembles human skin after it's been badly burned. The story Merlin told is chilling: In his former home he lived with a 13-year-old and a 14-year-old boy. One boy held Merlin while the other poured acid down his back. The boys also tried to dock Merlin's tail by tying a rubber band tightly around the base of it.

Merlin was allowed to wander freely and a neighbor called animal control because Merlin was rooting around in the trash. When the animal control officer saw evidence of abuse, he took Merlin to the shelter. The shelter vet removed the rubber band and amputated the tail.

Despite this history of abuse, Merlin is a wonderful dog, says Tania. He still likes to wander—it was a major form of entertainment for him in his old life, since that was how he occupied his time. He asked Tania to respect his desire to wander and the two struck a deal: late at night, she would allow him to wander for only 20 minutes. At the end of the 20-minute period, Tania, who keeps an eye on the clock, tele-pathically communicates that time's up and Merlin comes home.

Tania's a responsible dog person and wouldn't ordinarily feel com-fortable letting a dog wander. But she doesn't worry about Merlin. "I am totally confident about letting him out," she says. "He has reas-sured me through Patty that he will be okay. He knows the dangers and knows how to take care of himself."

On a few occasions, Tania has let Merlin out in the morning and he has not returned immediately as usual. She's had to take the time to locate him and bring him in the house, putting her behind sched-ule for taking her daughter to school. Each time that's happened, the delay has kept Tania out of harm's way. As she proceeded on her way later than usual, she would discover that she'd avoided a four-car traf-fic accident, for example. "Merlin is very intuitive," she says.

Michele Hegedus used the services of Gail De Sciose to help her after she adopted a shelter cat. Touché, an orange tabby cat, was com-pletely overwhelmed by the shelter environment when Michele adopted him. "If he could have turned himself inside out, he would have," she recalls. The four-year-old cat was very shy and suffered from an upper respiratory infection. Michele was worried that his respira-tory problems would result in pneumonia, as often happens to many fearful shelter animals. She felt he needed quiet, and a lot of attention and care.

She called Gail to speak with Touché and learn more about his past. "I saw it as a unique opportunity to get his perspective," she says. Gail learned from Touché that he had been kept locked in a gray bathroom in the basement, where he was cared for (to the extent he was cared for) by a man. He'd been socially deprived and was afraid of men and men's voices. He didn't even know what to do with toys.

Touché had been through several homes because he wasn't socia-ble. But he found the right home with Michele. Armed with the knowledge of his past, Michele was able to give him the love and at-tention he needed, while slowly bringing him out of his shell. "Com-munication sessions are part of his socialization," she says. It took

Touché two years in his new home before he starting purring. You'd never know it to meet him. "I'm very fortunate, because he is now seven and he is just a love bug," says Michele.

Touché is very sensitive to loud sounds—even the telephone terrified him at first. When it rang, he would run under the bed and shake. His fear of the ringing telephone seemed strange until Michele learned that he had been isolated in a relatively soundproof environment, that basement bathroom. Rather than get exasperated by this behavior, Michele realized that she needed to be very calm when the phone rang and let him know that it didn't alarm her at all. After a few months, rather than run away when the phone rang, he instead stopped what he was doing and looked to Michele as if to ask, "What do you want me to do?" Now he races to the phone when it rings and brings Michele a toy so that she can play with him while she talks.

Think of all the fascinating things you could learn about your companion animal if you could talk to him about his past. Your best friend's secrets are only a session away.

Chapter 6

Getting Your Animals' Help with Big Decisions

Keeping your animal friend informed of what's going on and reassuring him when times get difficult is an important way animal communication can help you. Many people use animal communicators to let their animals know when they are going on vacation, for example, and what will happen when they're gone.

Ginny Debbink says that animals invariably know when their people are leaving for a trip. Since I've become wise to the fact that our animals understand us when we speak to them, I make a big point of explaining to Kramer and Scout if I have to leave them overnight. I tell them where I'm going, how long I'll be gone and count out how many mornings they'll wake up before I come home. Thinking it was easier on the dogs, I used to pack on the sly and try to slink away as if nothing unusual were happening, but Ginny taught me that my animals would rather know exactly what to expect than to be hoodwinked.

Whenever something important is happening, being able to talk with your animal friends about it can go a long way toward relieving your animals' anxiety—and your own. "I ask my animal companions' opinion when making decisions ranging from the simple (such as their food preferences) to the profound (their preference for medical treatment or euthanasia)," says Susan Rifkin Ajamian, a regular client of Anita Curtis. "It is comforting to know that when making major decisions I have been able to consider their wishes."

Animal communication can be a big help in emergencies. It allows you to apprise your animals of what's going on so that they're not utterly befuddled. Mary Malone had already left her Greyhound, Kate, in a kennel for eight days when she went on vacation to Montana. But when she arrived back home in Wilmington, N.C., and got off the plane, Mary had a stroke. She was rushed to the hospital, where she stayed for ten days. Kate continued to stay at the kennel.

One of Gail De Sciose's clients, Electa Brown, is a friend of Mary's and suggested she contact Gail and ask her to communicate with Kate to let her know what was going on. Mary was concerned about caring for Kate when she came home from the hospital. Kate's a docile dog who is easy to look after, but usually she sulks after she's been left at the kennel. Mary was afraid that Kate would be frightened of the walker that Mary had to use when she first came home and was very concerned that Kate might pull on the leash, which would prevent Mary from being able to walk her.

So Gail spoke with Kate. When Mary and her daughter went to pick Kate up after spending nearly a month at the kennel, Kate behaved beautifully. She didn't go through her usual sulking routine. She wasn't afraid of the walker or the cane and she didn't pull on the leash. Mary noticed a marked improvement over the behavior she had feared. "Certainly she was different from how she usually is."

EXPLAINING HEALTH CARE

Joan Bosia, a client of Gail De Sciose, had a tiny zebra finch named Fluffy who was very sick. The veterinarians feared that Fluffy had cancer, but when Gail tuned into Fluffy, the little bird told her that she didn't have cancer. After Joan relayed Gail's description of how Fluffy felt, the vet was able to determine that she was suffering from a systemic infection. One of her legs and feet became atrophied and gnarled and the vet thought it should be amputated.

Gail spoke with Fluffy about the amputation. She asked the little 2 $1/2$-inch-long bird how she felt about the amputation and how Joan could best help her heal. Fluffy opted for the amputation. "She wasn't afraid," says Joan. "She knew I'd be there throughout the entire procedure." When Gail spoke with Fluffy the morning of the surgery, the little bird was gung-ho. "Let's do it!" she said.

Joan kept up a running commentary for Fluffy throughout every aspect of the procedure (including when Fluffy was under the anesthetic). Joan explained out loud everything that was occurring.

Fluffy has recovered beautifully from the surgery and from her illness. "She is happy, healthy and growing all her feathers back," says an ebullient Joan. She adds, "Gail was instrumental in guiding me through the process."

ADDING NEW MEMBERS TO YOUR ANIMAL FAMILY

Bringing more than one animal under one roof, be they the same or different species, can make for a wonderful menagerie. But animals are individuals; they can have personality conflicts. One great way to use animal communication to your benefit is to check with your animals before bringing newcomers in. You can make sure that the resident animals are comfortable with the idea of a new family member and introduce the new animal before she even arrives.

Stacy Vornbrock has learned through Sonya Fitzpatrick that her cats like to see a picture of any new animal before he is brought into the house. When she went to a shelter to pick out a new kitten to join the family, she sent a mental image to her cats of the little kitty, whom she named Louis. He was greeted with open arms. (Stacy even sends images of new furniture so that her cats will be comfortable when it arrives.)

One of her cats, Samuel, was so enamored of Louis that Stacey was concerned that the big cat might hurt the little kitten. "He was Louis's big, black shadow," recalls Stacey, and so she asked Sonya to speak with Samuel. "I would never hurt the kitten!" Samuel said. He never did.

UNHAPPY BEDFELLOWS

Even if you don't use animal communication to grease the wheels of your new animal's arrival, it can help with problems after the animals are already in residence. But sometimes the best an animal communicator can do is to let you know that a situation is simply untenable for the animal or animals, and that adjustments have to be made.

Taffy is a beloved orange tabby cat who lives with Lisa and Rob Papp. Lisa and Rob felt that Taffy would enjoy a feline companion and adopted a young cat they named Tinker. From the outset (after Tinker was comfortable enough to come out from under the bed), the situation wasn't good. Tinker was relentless in her harassment of poor Taffy, and Taffy was miserable.

By the end of six months, Taffy became ill and could barely walk. He'd lost the energy to jump up onto a chair and was in an unhealthy mental state. He even suffered a concussion from running into a door trying to get away from Tinker. The veterinarian treated the symptoms, but it took Gail De Sciose to figure out what the real cause of the illness was: Tinker.

Lisa told Taffy, "We thought you wanted a friend." Taffy succinctly replied, "You were wrong." Taffy liked the family just the way it was—before Tinker joined it. "It's not that she's a bad sort," Taffy said of Tinker. "It's just that she doesn't belong here."

Lisa and Rob felt they had no choice but to find a new home for Tinker, as much as it went against their conviction that, once adopted, animals should be kept for their entire lifetime. Lisa regretted not having done it sooner. "I feel so bad," she says. "Here my little baby [Taffy] was half dead and I was still hanging on to my 'I would never give up a pet' dictum."

In any case, Gail spoke with Tinker and explained the situation. She told her that she needed to go to a home where she was considered a blessing. Tinker understood and said she wanted to live with a family where there was someone home all day and that living with another cat would be fine.

The Papps took Tinker to adoption day with a local rescue group. That day a family arrived looking for an exact twin to the cat they already had. Tinker was identical. The family even worked at home, so Tinker's wish list was met.

The rescue group enforces a 48-hour waiting period before taking home an adoptee, so Tinker came back home and lived with Taffy for two more days. Out loud, Lisa told them exactly what was going on, that Tinker was here for two days only, and then would be moving elsewhere.

For the first time, Tinker's harassment of Taffy stopped. And the day before Tinker left, Taffy walked right up to her (a first) and started licking her forehead. Tinker protested a little, and Taffy put his paw on her forehead and persisted. "Taffy wanted to show her there were no hard feelings," says Lisa.

Lisa and Tinker's story illustrates an important point. If you find that you really must find a new home for your animal friend, for whatever reason, it is so important for you to explain to the animal what is happening. Let him know where he's going and why he needs to leave. And be sure and tell him that you appreciate what he did for you and how he will contribute in his new home. This simple task (you can do it out loud—you don't have to hire an animal communicator) can go a long way toward counteracting any feelings of rejection and confusion your animal friend might be experiencing. And that, in turn, will make you feel better.

In a similar vein, Nancy Roberts had two dogs who simply didn't get along. It was clear that Shepherd-mix Chynna simply couldn't tolerate the newcomer to the family, Golden Retriever Keegan. But rather than being the victim, like Taffy was, Chynna was the aggressor. She would attack Keegan whenever she was given the chance, so Nancy was forced to keep them separated and live a life negotiating baby gates.

Nancy spoke to Chynna about Keegan through Ginny Debbink. Chynna said that she didn't know why, but whenever she saw Keegan, she was just filled with rage and wanted to kill him. "I can't help it," she said. "When I see him I can't stop myself." This was rather surprising coming from a dog who tolerates the puppies that Nancy raises for Guide Dogs for the Blind. But Chynna offered no solutions. She said that she could just not bring herself to act differently.

Nancy checked to see how Keegan felt about the situation. He said that he was afraid that Chynna was going to kill him and he didn't like living in fear.

Because Chynna joined the family first and because as a dog-aggressive dog, she would be a problem to place, Nancy decided that Keegan should be found a new home. He said he understood and that though he didn't want to leave, he thought it would be best if he were found a home where he didn't have to be afraid. With the help of the rescue group through which Nancy originally obtained Keegan, he was found a wonderful new home where he enjoys only-dog stature.

That animal communication session was a huge help for Nancy, who had found herself in an unmanageable situation. "It has given me a sense of peace," she says. "It was hard to let Keegan go, but a little while after he was gone, I could see that it was the right decision. The household has relaxed. I didn't have to stay on my guard." The stress of fearing that the safety systems would fail and somehow the two dogs would come face to face and hurt one another was alleviated.

Nancy did tell Chynna that she would not tolerate any perceived ability to kick another dog out of the house. "I won't let you do this again," she told her dog. "You can't just think you can kick dogs out of the household when you want to."

IS YOUR ANIMAL IN THE RIGHT HOME?

Susan Kalev, who lives in New York City, has a cat who yearns to be outside. Susan walks Soho on a leash, but when he's inside, the cat spends a good deal of time scratching at the door asking to go out. Susan started to think that maybe Soho would be happier in a home in the country where he could more safely spend time outdoors.

Susan knew, however, that because Soho is disabled (he's deaf and has impaired vision) the country wouldn't be particularly safe for him either. She asked Gail De Sciose to ask him if he'd like to move to a new home in the country.

Soho wanted to have his cake and eat it too. "He said he would like to be with me in the country," Susan recalls. Gail explained that with his disabilities there's a good chance that his life would be shortened if he were allowed to go outside. He said that he didn't care about safety; he wanted to be free.

Susan began the process of looking for a new home for Soho. But she was pleasantly surprised: As she continued to check in with him through Gail, she learned that he had become more accepting of his indoor, city-cat lifestyle. Soho happily remains with her in Manhattan.

EASING THE DIFFICULTY OF RELOCATING

Peg Banks had come to a difficult time in her life. She and her companion of many years had split up and Peg moved with her dogs to the home of friends who owned a kennel. One of her dogs stayed in the house with her, but the other three stayed in the kennel runs. This was particularly hard on Courtney, a mixed-breed dog whom Peg had adopted after Courtney had spent her first seven years in a laundry room. Courtney had been with Peg for only two years and they were still working at establishing a bond. After seven years in a small room, being placed in a kennel run was more than poor Courtney could handle.

She started regressing. She became wild-eyed and trembling and shied away from human contact. She would wail when put back in the run. Peg put her on valium, which seemed to dull the light in her eyes without helping her cope.

Peg—in her first experience with a professional communicator—contacted her friend Ginny Debbink. Rather than her usual phone consultation, Ginny promised to contact Courtney during a private time and to let Peg know what she had said.

When Peg left Courtney in her kennel run at lunchtime shortly after contacting Ginny, Courtney was her same freaked-out self. But when Peg came back a few hours later, she knew instantly that Ginny had talked with Courtney. "She was calm, her eyes were alert," Peg recalls. And it wasn't the calm brought on by the valium. "She seemed like she was okay. She wasn't trembling or drooling."

Ginny had succeeded in reassuring Courtney that her whole life wasn't falling apart around her. She instructed Peg to constantly tell Courtney what was going to happen next. This would, she said, help Courtney be more at ease.

That running commentary not only helped Courtney, it helped Peg. "I'm sure I had projected all my fears on my dogs," says Peg. By taking life one moment at a time and reassuring the dogs about it, Peg was able to calm herself and help her dogs feel better in turn. Peg took Courtney off the valium after the conversation with Ginny and the dog did fine.

Peg, who is extremely close with all four of her dogs, doesn't see using the services of an animal communicator as something she would do on a routine basis. She doesn't feel the need to hire a communicator to help her get to know her animals better. But she does use Ginny's services during stressful times, when she feels the need to get some vital information through to her animals. "I see it more as an EMT kind of thing," she says.

When Helen MacKinnon moved to North Carolina from New Jersey she was particularly concerned about it being difficult for her nine cats. Her move to New Jersey some years before had been tough: "It really did a number on my Maine Coon's immune system," Helen recalls.

So this time, she asked Gail De Sciose to speak with her cats and explain what was happening. The head cat, George, was selected as the spokescat for the other felines. Gail spoke with him and he relayed the information to the other cats. When the move was completed, "It was as if they had always been here," says Helen.

COPING WITH SEPARATION ANXIETY (BOTH ANIMAL AND HUMAN)

Both Susan Goldstein and her parrot MacMillan, suffered separation anxiety whenever Susan had to travel without MacMillan. She would take him with her on trips whenever it was safe, but on occasion security concerns forced her to leave him at home.

In anticipation of one such trip, Susan contacted Gail De Sciose and asked for help. Gail talked with MacMillan and explained that Susan was leaving but that she would be back. Gail told the parrot that Susan was worried about how he was going to do in her absence, both emotionally and physically (the bird, who ordinarily flies freely in the house has to spend more time in a cage when Susan is gone).

Susan and Gail asked MacMillan's permission for her to take the trip. "He never had separation anxiety again after that," says Susan. The fact that MacMillan was no longer upset helped Susan's emotions as well. "I know that he is clear that if I ever have to leave him, it is necessary," she says.

Susan said that she watched MacMillan during that session with Gail. "I knew that she was getting through, because of his body language." This experience was a key motivator in Susan's decision to include animal communication in the holistic veterinary practice that she owns with her husband, Bob Goldstein.

GETTING INPUT ON REPRODUCTIVE DECISIONS

Animal communication can allow you to include your animal friends in making major decisions about their lives. Vicky Carpenter's Scottish Terrier, Ceihlin, had a difficult time reproducing. Her first litter was reabsorbed and only two of the puppies in her second litter, both male, survived. Ceihlin is a wonderful example of her breed and Vicky really wanted a girl puppy from her, so she asked Ceihlin whether she would be willing to be bred again. Ceihlin said that her immune system isn't healthy enough to reproduce, so she didn't want to be bred.

Vicky had her spayed immediately and simply dropped her dream of a girl puppy from Ceihlin.

USING ANIMAL COMMUNICATION TO EASE LIFE CHANGES

Nancy Roberts raises puppies for Guide Dogs for the Blind. Saying goodbye to the puppies as they go back to the school for training for their life's work is always bittersweet. One of the puppies, a German Shepherd Dog named Detroit, had especially captured Nancy's heart, and she requested that she be given the opportunity to adopt him if he should be cut from the program for some reason.

Detroit was Nancy's third guide-dog puppy. When it was time for him to go back to school, she contacted Ginny Debbink and asked her to tell him what was going to happen to him. "I was worried he'd think that I was just abandoning him," she said. Nancy and Gail explained why he was going away and what he would be doing. Detroit said he understood, since he'd heard Nancy explaining to other people that he was a guide-dog-in-training. He said he wasn't so sure that he wanted to do the work, but since he knew it was important for Nancy, he would try his best.

Well, Detroit didn't make the grade in training. "He is too environmentally aware," says Nancy, "too edgy." When the school decided to send him back to Nancy to live, she asked Ginny to contact him again, while he was en route, to tell him where he was going. "He is a little confused, but happy to find out that he going to see you," Ginny told Nancy. Detroit also reassured Nancy that he wasn't too disappointed about not becoming a guide dog. "He worked hard, and gave it his best try, but he never was sure it was right for him to begin with," Ginny said.

Nancy also used Ginny's services when it came to making a decision about where her cat, MacKenzie, would live. Nancy's roommate, Heather, had become very close with MacKenzie in the two years that they'd lived together. Heather was moving to another state and

Nancy and Heather thought that perhaps MacKenzie would prefer to make the move with her. It was an agonizing decision, as Nancy had had the 15-year-old tabby since she was a little kitten and would miss her dearly.

So they went to the source and asked MacKenzie what her preference was. MacKenzie said that she would miss Nancy, but that "Heather had always needed her more." (Heather and MacKenzie had become close while Heather recovered from a number of knee surgeries.)

The session confirmed Nancy's hunch. "It was comforting for me to know that MacKenzie wanted to go, so I didn't feel like I was abandoning her or sending her away when she'd rather stay." But Heather did need the kitty, so the decision was made. Without the session with Ginny, Nancy would have worried over whether she'd done the right thing.

As these stories show, getting the input of the animals themselves can be extremely beneficial when an important decision that will affect their welfare needs to be made. The animals and their humans can enter a new phase of life confident that they've done the right thing for all parties.

Chapter 7

Communicate to Help Solve Behavior Problems

When your animal companion behaves in inexplicable and problematic ways and your best efforts to solve the problem don't help, animal communication just might do the trick. It allows you to ask your animal why he's doing something that troubles you. And perhaps equally as important, you can explain why the behavior is a concern for you. Then you can formulate a plan (or negotiate a solution) to get past the problem.

Bear in mind that talking to your animal doesn't turn him into an angel overnight. "Just because you can explain to him doesn't mean they won't screw up," says Dawn Hayman. You can, after all, communicate with a child or a teenager, but that doesn't mean she'll mind what you have to say. A conversation doesn't ensure instant understanding. But it is a great tool.

The simple act of listening to an animal can pay dividends. "It is amazing when the animal gets to be heard," says Patty Summers. "Once they've been listened to they often truly change their behavior from that point on."

I have a couple of behavior problems with Kramer and Scout that I've spoken with them about. The first one, barking and lunging on leash when seeing big, black dogs at a distance, was a big issue for us. Together my two Standard Poodles outweigh me and it was difficult for me to control them when they were in full-blown hysteria. I feel foolish when it happens and I get very angry. It was truly having a negative impact on our daily outings together.

So I talked about it with them through Ginny Debbink. And I learned a few things. I learned that they're acting out of fear. That hadn't crossed my mind (though it seems so obvious now), since they certainly don't look scared. But they're trying to fend off these scary looking dogs (never mind that Kramer and Scout are big, black dogs themselves). Kramer explained that he must try to scare away any dog he feels he couldn't beat up if pushed. This explains why the smaller dogs weren't a problem. And why, on the rare instances when they actually came close to the objects of their fear (most of the people with the dogs they barked at wanted nothing to do with us), they weren't aggressive.

I've learned that this isn't at all unusual. Underneath the mask of aggression in most dogs, says Patty Summers, is fear. The best defense is a good offense is the mindset at work. In other words, they put on a very brave, scary front in an effort to avoid confrontation.

Ginny explained to them how difficult their behavior was for me to handle. Kramer promised to try to hold himself together, if I would reassure him that the dog wouldn't hurt us and that I would take care of the situation. Prior to our discussion with Ginny, I would skulk away from approaching scary dogs or try to hide behind a tree so my dogs wouldn't see the oncoming dog. Of course, the Poodles always saw the other dog and by trying to avoid the situation, I was simply validating their idea that these dogs were to be feared.

Kramer did appear to make a real effort not to go ballistic. But it was impossible for him to do so when Scout would start barking. So Ginny spoke with Scout. She explained that I would like her to stop the barking and lunging. Scout—who's not big on compromise, I've discovered—said that she was sorry, but she didn't think she would be able to change the behavior. Then Ginny told her that Kramer had made a promise to his mom and that she was making it impossible for him to keep that promise. Reluctantly, she said, "Okay, I'll do it for Kramer."

That very next day their promises were put to the acid test. As we left the park on our morning stroll, we encountered our nemeses: a pair of Rottweilers who walk with a man who taunts me about my dogs' bad behavior. (His Rotties are always perfectly behaved.) My blood pressure rises when I think about him, let alone see him. As we walked out of the park gate, there they were, not 20 feet away.

It was the moment of truth. I took a deep breath, told the Poodles in an upbeat voice not to worry, that those dogs were not going to bother us, and we took a sharp right turn and walked briskly away from them. Sweet Scout didn't say a word. Kramer let out a couple of relatively calm barks. We walked a short distance at heel, I asked them to sit, and I very nearly wept, I was so grateful and proud of my dogs for keeping their promise under pressure.

Whenever I check in with the dogs through Ginny, we touch base about how we're doing with the big, black dogs. I wish I could say that their behavior is perfect. But animal communication isn't a magic wand. What it has given me is an understanding of the dogs' motivation, as well as some tools to cope with the behavior. I do my best to visualize success: As we walk past oncoming dogs I try my hardest to picture Kramer and Scout walking calmly by. Scout tells me that I'm not very successful in this positive visualization (I just can't seem to help but picture them going nuts), but I keep trying. And with every success, my confidence increases and paranoia decreases and, one year later, taking a walk is a lot more pleasurable for all three of us.

To be candid, I'll admit that I also have a situation where (so far, anyway) animal communication hasn't been able to help. Kramer, who is a very nice, non-destructive dog in all other environments (except around big, black dogs), goes nuts in the car. I'm talking berserk. Before we started muzzling him in the car two years ago, he would tear apart the upholstery. We've replaced the front seat once, its head-rest twice, and two door panels. The other two door panels still have bites taken out of them. He also barks and whines and salivates and can't possibly sleep a wink in the car. If he weren't safely belted, he'd be running all over the back seat.

This behavior, which began when he was about six months old, has been the topic of much discussion between my husband and me. Does he like the car or does he hate it? He's incredibly excited about getting in the car. He just loses his mind once he's in.

It was literally the first question I ever asked Kramer through an animal communicator. I learned that his senses are overwhelmed in the car. The sounds are too loud, the smells too stinky, everything's a blur. He's just reacting to his sensory overload.

Thinking this was my big chance, I asked him what I could do to alleviate the stress of the car ride and facilitate better behavior. His re-sponse: "I am open to any suggestions you have. I'm perfectly willing to work with you to make the car a more pleasant place." But he of-fered no solutions. So it's up to me to come up with ideas and so far nothing we've tried has helped. I've talked to him about this problem with several communicators and he consistently explains the situa-tion, but can never come up with a solution (beyond one I can't af-ford: buying a bigger car that would accommodate his crate, then covering his crate like a bird cage).

I feel better knowing a little bit about what's going through his mind (even though it appears he's lost his mind), but I am disappointed that animal communication hasn't afforded us a solution. That might be the case with your problem. But then again, there may be a simple solution waiting for you just by asking your animal.

SURPRISING ANSWERS

If you talk with your animal through an animal communicator in order to get to the bottom of a behavior problem, you might just be surprised at what you learn. Sometimes the behavior seems so myste-rious, yet there's a simple explanation.

Mary Jane Monahan's German Shepherd, Shebah, was a fearful puppy who grew up to be a fearful dog. Mostly her fear is directed toward strange people, but she also had a very negative reaction to an inanimate object: garbage cans. When Mary Jane would take Shebah for a walk on garbage-collection day, the German Shepherd would attack and actually bite the cans. Mary Jane had a session with Ginny Debbink and asked Shebah about this mysterious conduct. For whatever reason, Shebah believed that there were people hiding inside of the garbage cans. So Mary Jane walked up to the can, lifted the lid and showed her that there were no people hiding there. Shebah's fear subsided and the garbage can attacks ceased.

In another surprising case, Diane Beuthe unraveled the secret of her horse Toy's manic behavior when trailered. Of course, it's very important for horses to be able to go into a trailer and ride comfortably, just as it is important for a dog or a cat to be able to ride in the car.

This was a big issue for Diane, as she and her husband were moving from New Jersey to Florida with six horses. Toy wouldn't hesitate to enter the trailer (in which he would ride with a partner). But once in, he would lean on his side against the center divider and scramble his four legs against the wall. This was not an acceptable arrangement when there are supposed to be two horses in the trailer. Once, he did it while his partner Magic was in the trailer and brought her down with him, causing injury to both of them.

Diane asked Nancy Mueller if she could get to the bottom of the problem. Toy told Nancy that he was convinced that once the wall of the trailer had hit him. Diane assumes that the trailer had hit a bump and Toy had been thrown against the wall. Or perhaps he had nodded off and fallen against the wall (she's quite certain that the wall didn't actually move and hit him). Nancy explained that the wall wasn't going to hurt him. She and Diane also worked with flower essences and other healing techniques, and now Toy trailers just fine. "He went from being a horse who couldn't go three-quarters of a mile in the trailer to one who can travel between New Jersey and Florida," says Diane.

AGGRESSION PROBLEMS

I mentioned earlier that Mary Jane Monahan's dog Shebah was fearful of people. If only this fear of people were as simple to resolve as her fear of garbage cans. Mary Jane learned through Ginny Debbink that Shebah is so attached to her that she's afraid of a stranger taking Mary Jane away from her. When they're out walking, Mary Jane must always be on the alert and at the ready with a distracting treat when strangers walk by (the pair live in New York City, so there are a lot of strangers walking by), to prevent Shebah from lunging at people. Mary Jane learned that Shebah perceives her shifting of posture and attention to be fear on Mary Jane's part, which makes Shebah all the more fearful. "She said that I arrange myself differently when I see a stranger," says Mary Jane. And she reacts by trying to keep strangers away because she feeds off of Mary Jane's nervousness. It's a vicious cycle.

Since the communication session, "I try not to get so nervous when strangers approach," says Mary Jane. She also takes Ginny's advice and before leaving on a walk visualizes a peaceful stroll with no threats. "I picture us sitting and letting strangers walk by." Shebah's had a few setbacks since the consultation with Ginny, but for the most part the understanding Mary Jane gained through Ginny has helped her manage Shebah's fearful aggression.

Sherry Moore has a Doberman named Niko who growled and snapped at her. Sherry now sees that the traditional, dominating training techniques she'd used with him contributed to the behavior ("I lost his trust"), as did the fact that he was taken away from his litter at only 5 weeks old and didn't have a chance to develop acceptable pack behavior from his mom and littermates.

Sherry consulted Patty Summers and learned that Niko's growling was a form of communication. It was the way he let it be known that he was unhappy. Niko also revealed that he was unsure of what was expected of him (Sherry shows him in obedience), which made him fearful because of the punishment he'd received in the past. When he was afraid, he'd growl.

Working with Patty, they were able to reach compromises, as Patty told Sherry the things that rewarded Niko. Sherry learned to reward him for good behavior and ignore bad behavior.

Niko now has his Companion Dog obedience title. "Without Patty's help," says Sherry, "I would have thought that Niko was being a vicious dog and put him to sleep." Sherry's heart told her that that wasn't the answer and with Patty's help, and that of the holistic veterinarian who referred her to Patty, she found solutions to her problems.

"Niko is not aggressive," Patti discovered. "I consider him a confused child, but once he understands something [is a problem behavior], he doesn't do it again."

Diane Beuthe took in a horse who consistently threw her riders. This horse, Magic, had a definite attitude. Diane was able to break Magic of the habit of throwing her, but she didn't care for the horse's willful ways. She asked Nancy Mueller to talk with Magic and explain that this was really her last shot. She'd been through a number of homes and with her attitude she just wasn't going to be welcome in another one. "Either she had to straighten up and fly right or she'd end up in a can of dog food," says Diane. Nancy spoke with Magic, who understood what she was being told, but asserted her own opinion, too. "She said, 'This is a partnership and you need to give 50 percent too,'" says Diane.

The two worked out a partnership arrangement (which Diane says is kind of like a marriage) and five years later Magic is a happy horse with a job to do. Diane and her husband are very involved in fox hunting. Diane's role is to help the huntsman with working the hounds. She rides Magic when she does this, so Magic stays very focused on the hounds. If one of them breaks ranks with the pack, she retrieves the hound without being asked. "She's very good at what she does," says Diane.

PHYSICAL ORIGINS OF BEHAVIOR PROBLEMS

Many behavior problems are actually physical in origin. For example, aggression is often the result of the animal being in pain. A chiropractor can frequently help—Dawn Hayman makes many refer-rals to a veterinary chiropractor. "I've seen chiropractic turn so many aggressive animals around," she says. "Most really sound-sensitive dogs, in particular, can benefit. If they have some cervical vertebrae that are out of alignment, they will hear things more loudly."

Electa Brown sought the help of Gail De Sciose for her Papillon, Ty. In 1996, poor Ty had been the victim of a mean-spirited bully, a large man who kicked her one day while Electa was walking her down the street in New York City. Ty was clearly in pain, but nothing showed up on the x-rays her veterinarian took. Each year, Ty became more and more fearful of people. When Electa contacted Gail, three years after the incident, she was at the end of her rope; Ty became hys-terical even around familiar people, such as Electa's boyfriend.

When Gail connected with Ty, she learned that Ty had terrible pain in her neck that radiated down her front left leg. That pain, coupled with the trauma of having been hurt by a stranger (and the trauma of watching her mom confront her attacker) made Ty very wary of any human's touch (except Electa's). She didn't bite, unless cornered, but she barked at people and wouldn't let them anywhere near her.

Gail suggested that Ty see a veterinary chiropractor, who con-firmed everything that Gail had said. Ty suffered from damaged cer-vical vertebrae. The chiropractic adjustments were ultimately very beneficial, though they were painful at first. Gail helped Ty understand the pain so that she would allow the chiropractor to treat her. Gail ex-plained that the treatments might hurt now, but that she would feel better down the road if she gave it some time. Ty understood and al-lowed the chiropractor to work on her. The chiropractic eventually did the trick. "She's fine now," says a grateful Electa Brown.

Carol Albino had a horse, Buddy, who was unpredictable. He had hurt her on many occasions, by bucking and the like. In fact, he hurt her so badly that she sold him. And he continued to hurt his new people.

Carol sponsored an event with Lydia Hiby, inviting all the horses she'd "ever put a leg over" to her farm to have a communication session. Of course, this included Buddy. Lydia discovered that Buddy had absolutely no peripheral vision. For horses, who are prey animals, keeping tabs on their surroundings is vital. Living without peripheral vision is like going through life with blinders on—it must have made poor Buddy feel defenseless, says Carol. All of a sudden his unpredictable behavior made a lot more sense.

"We now try to give horses the benefit of the doubt when we have a problem," she says. "First we call the vet, then we call Lydia to try to get to the root of the problem."

Anita Curtis had a client whose horse stopped before the first jump every time he was asked to jump. Anita was able to pinpoint the unexpected source of the problem: The horse's tooth hurt him. He told her that he stopped before the first jump in order to clench his teeth so that the jolt of the landing wouldn't hurt him further. Prior to the onset of the problem, a dentist accidentally had broken one the horse's teeth. They fixed the broken tooth and the horse went back to winning his jumping competitions regularly.

Amy Nowak was introduced to animal communication when she had a problem with her horse, Sophie. She was asking Sophie to gait differently. Amy wanted Sophie to bring her hind end under, which caused her back to come up. Every time she asked her to do that, however, Sophie would stop and swing her head around and look at Amy's leg as she sat in the saddle. "I realized she was trying to tell me something, but I didn't know what." Her trainer suggested she contact Dawn Hayman.

Sophie told Dawn that the saddle hurt her back when she brought her back up as Amy asked. She had no muscle across the top of her rib heads, so there was no padding to prevent the pain of the saddle. By stopping and looking at Amy's leg, she was doing her best to point at the saddle and let Amy know that it didn't fit properly. The solution was simple; Amy bought a custom saddle and the problem was fixed. From that point on, Amy was hooked on animal communication.

HELP IN THE OBEDIENCE RING

Michael McCarthy and his partner Brian Miller enjoy participating in a variety of activities with their enthusiastic Chesapeake Bay Retriever, Quaid, including hunting field tests and obedience trials. Quaid did well in the obedience ring, except on the 10-minute down-stays with the handler out of sight. Although he could perform the down-stay in practice at obedience class, in the ring he inevitably broke the stay and went to visit other dogs in competition (which certainly didn't make him popular with the other dogs' handlers). Because of this habit, Quaid couldn't advance in obedience competition, and Michael and Brian were on the verge of quitting competitive obedience altogether.

When Michael spoke to Quaid with Gail De Sciose, he asked Quaid why he couldn't hold his down stay in competition. Quaid said, "I just can't control my urge to say hello to the other dogs in the ring."

Michael endured minutes of silence on the phone while Gail explained to Quaid that his visiting made it difficult for him to succeed in the obedience ring and that his dads would like him to try to refrain from doing it. By the end of that five minutes, Quaid said that he now understood how important it was to his dads and that he would do his best to try not to visit when he was under a command.

Less than a week later, Quaid competed in an obedience match. He kept his word. To the delight and amazement of Michael and Brian and Quaid's teacher, he held the stay—for the first time ever in competition. "Quaid knew what we wanted him to do, he just didn't know how important it was to us and that he would be able to do more fun stuff down the road once we got past this level of competition," says Michael. "This made the session worth its weight in gold!"

Performance problems with dogs who compete in various sports are not unusual. In fact, Patty Summers teams up with dog trainer Catherine Mills to offer combined training and animal communication clinics to help obedience dogs work through some of their performance issues.

This marriage of dog training and animal communication is quite unusual. Although positive reinforcement methods of dog training are becoming more popular, the traditional methods were based on showing a dog who's boss, an attitude that doesn't resonate in the world of animal communication where both human and animal share their thoughts and feelings.

"I do understand why conventional training methods are used," says Patty of those methods that put the human in the role of the "alpha" dog by rolling the dog on the back or shaking them by the scruff. "But a dog knows you are not a dog." Patty says you can be a leader without being a dominant being. "We lead by gaining respect for one another."

One of the ways that animal communication helps with behavior problems is that it changes the way a person looks at her misbehaving animal friend. Sometimes she gets stuck in a mindset that an animal (particularly a dog or a horse) should do what she wants. Period. An animal communicator can change that and help the person look at the problem from her animal's perspective. "Until people stop thinking in terms of owning their animals and teaching them commands, the same issue will continue to come up time and time again," says Ginny.

At one of their clinics, Patty and Catherine helped a client named Vicky Carpenter with her Scottish Terrier Seelie's problem. Like Quaid, the dog performed beautifully in practice sessions, but during a competition, she out and out refused to drop into a down when given the hand signal, a requirement in this level of obedience competition. Vicky didn't understand why Seelie, who clearly understood the signal, wouldn't perform it in the ring. So Patty asked her.

It turned out that Seelie, who has very healthy self-esteem and looks upon herself as a queen, found the hand signal, given in a public place, rude and demeaning. It was similar to how a waiter feels about a patron snapping his fingers at him.

Through Patty, Vicky and Seelie worked out a solution. If Vicky would drop her eyes when she raised her hand, it would be less offensive to Seelie and she would perform the exercise. Vicky kept her

69

end of the bargain and they haven't had a problem since. "Patty is literally responsible for that dog getting her obedience title," says Vicky.

Lydia Hiby talks with a lot of show animals (horses, dogs and cats) whose people want to make sure they enjoy showing. They also contact Lydia when there are problems in the show ring that they want to get the bottom of. Lydia says that if the animal truly doesn't enjoy showing, the person will often retire him. Or they'll strike a deal: If the animal completes a certain number of shows (or a title), he can retire. Or he can take a break from showing for a while and go out and get dirty. These negotiations, which Lydia calls "contracts" can go a long way toward keeping the animal happy. "Some show animals never get to experience what it is like to truly be an animal," says Lydia. "They can usually deal with it as long they can work out some sort of contract."

WHEN THE PROBLEM IS THE PERSON

When you use the services of an animal communicator, you may find that the problem is actually inside of you, not your animal friend. He's just trying to tell you about it. "I find more often than not that an animal's behavior is the result of the animal attempting to show the human a situation that is not working for the animal," says Sharon Callahan. When that's revealed, steps can be taken to address the problematic situation.

The emotions of our animals are inextricably intertwined with our own, which is why Sharon likes to treat both animal and human with flower essences (liquid preparations made from the life force of flowers used to heal on an emotional/spiritual level) following an animal communication consult.

Sonya Fitzpatrick sees this occurrence time and time again. "The majority of people come to me thinking they have an animal problem," she says. "When I talk with the animal, I find they have a people problem."

The animal communication session helps the human understand how the animal sees the world. "That is why I think animal communication is so important," says Sonya.

COMMUNICATING WITH NONDOMESTICATED ANIMALS

Telepathic communication isn't limited to domestic animals. Gail De Sciose has been hired to ask rodents to leave a house, for example.

Sonya Fitzpatrick's client Dorothy Fogle, who practices communicating with animals herself, once persuaded an armadillo who was digging up her plants to stop. Dorothy has expensive landscaping around her house on her Arabian horse farm in Texas and she caught an armadillo digging a big hole that led to a hiding place under the house and rooting up her plants. Dorothy's husband wanted her to shoot the wild animal. Instead, Dorothy dealt with it her own way. "I was sitting out one day and I knew the armadillo was in the big hole under the foundation. I told him telepathically to leave the landscaping alone." Dorothy told the armadillo he could live there, he just had to stop digging up the plants. "And do you know, I have not had one plant overturned since then!" she told me.

COMMUNICATING PRUDENTLY

When you speak to your animal you're silently sending him the feelings and images behind the words. Animal communicators assure me that our animals understand us. Silent or spoken aloud, all communication is telepathy, says Penelope Smith.

And sometimes they develop our sense of language. Gail De Sciose once spoke with a dog whose retort, when told he was beautiful, was, "You've got that right." That expression made the dog's person laugh because it's a phrase she uses all of the time.

Sometimes animals will describe themselves as their person describes them, says Anita Curtis. It's not unusual, for instance, for a dog to tell Anita, "I'm a good boy" after a lifetime of being told what a "good boy" he is.

But even when you're not speaking directly to your animal, he may be listening. Many animals will listen in on our conversations and keep abreast of the news of the household. Since I came to know that this was true, I've tried to be very careful about what I say about my dogs. I no longer tease them or say silly, insulting things because I think they don't understand.

An animal might hear something and act on it. At one point, Amy Nowak considered selling her horse, Sophie. She'd been offered a great deal of money for her and she thought that since she'd been so successful in helping solve Sophie's behavior problems that maybe she should go ahead and sell Sophie in order to make room for a rescue horse who needed rehabilitation.

All of a sudden, Sophie began misbehaving. "She reverted four years back in her training," recalls Amy. So Amy checked with Sophie through Dawn Hayman. Sophie made it very clear what was going on. "I heard that you were going to sell me, so I wanted to be bad so that no one would buy me." At that point, seeing how important it was to Sophie to stay with her, Amy abandoned all notions of selling her horse. And Sophie went back to being a well-behaved, well-trained horse.

Sometimes an animal is acting on a misunderstanding. He hears talk in the house, but since he's not explicitly included in the conversation, he may misinterpret information, which could lead to problem behavior. Such was the case for a client of Dawn Hayman. She called Dawn because her dog had begun to urinate and defecate in the house. When Dawn connected with the dog, she asked why she was doing this, despite the fact that she'd been trained to do her business outside.

Dawn was surprised to learn that the dog was actually acting on behalf of her person. It turns out that this family moves every 14 months and the move always causes a major disruption in their lives. The last move was so stressful it nearly gave the woman a nervous breakdown. It wasn't uncommon for the stress of the move to cause some housetraining lapses in the dog.

They had just found out that they were to move again after only a few months, but that they were guaranteed to stay at the next place for eight years. The dog caught wind that they were going to move again, but she hadn't heard the details. In the past she had also heard her mom say, "If she keeps ruining the carpet, we won't be able to sell the house." So she set out on a one-dog campaign to thwart the move by ruining the carpets and preventing the sale of the house.

Dawn explained to her client's dog that this move was actually a beneficial one for the family and that this was the last move they would make for a while. After that conversation, the dog did not have a single accident in the house.

YOU LOOK MAHVELOUS!

Sometimes our animals thwart us when we're trying to be the best caretakers we can and take care of health needs that might not be so pleasant for the animal. Electa Brown needed to brush her Papillon Ty's teeth. Ty had already had 11 teeth pulled, and brushing was a necessity. Like many dogs, Ty wanted no part of it. So Electa asked Gail to tell Ty why her mom needed to brush her teeth.

The way to a dog's heart must truly be through her stomach. Gail asked the little dog, "You like to eat, right?" Gail reminded her of the tooth removal and explained that if her teeth weren't brushed, she would lose more of them. And if more were to come out, she wouldn't be able to eat her favorite foods.

Such reasoning obviously worked. "It was like night and day," says Electa. The very next time she tried, Ty let her brush her teeth.

Like many dogs, Irish Terrier Michael does not like to have his nails clipped. Period. Michael was found in a local park as a young adult dog, so his person, Deborah Manheim, didn't have an opportunity to socialize him at a young age to having his feet handled. She knew the importance of short nails and tried frequently to cut them. Even getting one nail clipped was an ordeal.

Deborah spoke with Michael through Ginny Debbink. Michael said that he thought it was rude for anyone to touch his feet. ("I don't touch *your* feet," he said.) Ginny explained to Michael why it was important to let Deborah cut his nails. The very next day, Michael let Deborah cut three toenails.

PREVENTING PROBLEMS WITH COMMUNICATION

You can also use animal communication to try to prevent problems. Laura Watts has a young Doberman Pinscher named Grifter who absolutely adores Laura's father. They'd developed a greeting ritual that involved Grifter enthusiastically jumping up on his grandpa. But when Laura's father had open-heart surgery it was imperative that Grifter not jump on him. Three weeks after the operation, Laura held a party to which both her father and animal communicator Patty Summers were invited. Rather than banish Grifter to another room, Laura asked Patty to talk with him.

Before the father showed up, Patty spoke with Grifter and explained how very important it was for him not to jump, that his grandpa was recovering from surgery and that jumping on him could really hurt him.

The conversation worked—almost too well. When Laura's father walked in the house, Grifter not only didn't greet him, he went into the kitchen. Every time his grandpa would enter a room, Grifter would leave it. When the father went outside, Grifter came inside. He would not get within 12 feet of the recuperating man. "It was shocking," says Laura, "especially because this dog always jumped up on him and nibbled his beard." Patty tuned into to Grifter again and then told Laura, "I guess I overdid it a little; he's afraid of hurting your father."

After the parents left, Laura asked Patty to tell Grifter that they would let him know when it was all right to be near her father again. For three or four more visits, Grifter kept his distance. But after the father had healed, Laura told Grifter (out loud) that it was okay to greet him. He immediately went back to his exuberant greeting, complete with beard nibbling. Laura's parents had never bought into the idea of animal communication, she says. "They always thought I was a flake." After this experience, they said, "Maybe there is something to this animal communication thing!"

Chapter 8

Learning What Ails Your Animal

....

For the animal lover, there's not much worse than having a sick animal. In a sense, animal companions are like infants. We usually know when they're ill, but they don't have the language capabilities to tell us what's wrong (not out loud, anyway). Any parent whose infant has ever been sick knows the helplessness of trying to determine the best course of action. It's not much different for most people whose animals are sick, except when animal communication allows them to learn how the animal is feeling.

An animal communicator can help you know what ails your beloved animal friend. You may have a strong enough connection with him to find out for yourself, but many people have a difficult time communicating telepathically with their own animals at first. If you're just starting out and in urgent need of knowing how your animal friend feels physically, this is an opportune time to call in a professional animal communicator.

Many communicators actually feel what the animal is feeling. If the animal's front right paw is sore, for example, the communicator's right hand would hurt. Gail De Sciose once spoke with a cat who had throat cancer. Immediately, Gail's own mouth filled with sores. In another instance, she started shaking while speaking with a dog who had tremors.

A communicator need not have extensive knowledge of animal anatomy (in fact, Anita Curtis makes a point of not learning anatomy so she doesn't risk using scientific terms incorrectly). Most communicators simply report what they feel: a twinge in their own kidney area might signify a problem with the animal's kidney, for example.

Animals might send words or images or feelings as well. Once, when I asked Ginny Debbink to ask Kramer how he was feeling (he'd had a series of stomach upsets), he sent the color yellow. That night, he threw up copious amounts of yellow bile.

Most animal communicators are not veterinarians. Ethical communicators are very careful not to give specific diagnoses or veterinary advice. The Code of Ethics for Interspecies Animal Communicators, drawn up by Penelope Smith, explicitly states, "It is not our job to name and treat diseases, and we refer people to veterinarians for diagnosis of physical illness. We may relay animals' ideas, feelings, pains, symptoms, as they describe them or as we feel or perceive them, and this may be helpful to veterinary health professionals." (*See* Appendix B for the full text of the Code of Ethics.)

This point is very important to animal communicators and it bears repeating. Although they can be invaluable for helping you help your veterinarian assess what's wrong with your animal, animal communicators don't practice veterinary medicine. "I don't diagnose and I don't prescribe," declares Anita Curtis. Alice McClure agrees. "I don't feel it is my place to diagnose. It is not my purpose."

Although the animal communicator you work with will not diagnose the illness, the information she provides about how your animal is feeling can be very helpful to your veterinarian in making a diagnosis and in developing a treatment plan. "I usually get enough information from the animal to help the vet pinpoint the problem," says Sharon Callahan.

Of course, that assumes that your veterinarian will receive that information without rolling his or her eyes. Communicators tell me that animal communication is becoming more accepted among veterinarians, particularly those who practice holistic medicine. Many of the communicators I interviewed have veterinarians who call them to ask for information from a patient. Lydia Hiby has even had 14 veterinarians attend her workshops.

Several veterinarians call communicator Anita Curtis on a regular basis. One of those is Deborah Mack, a holistic vet in Boise, Idaho, who has attended animal communication seminars herself (her first was with Dawn Hayman). She says that although she can sometimes get a lot of information from an animal when she's not trying, she has some difficulty when she sets out to do it. "It's hard for me to get my left brain out of the way," she says. So when she needs some specific information from a patient, she gives Anita a call.

One such case was Milhouse, a spaniel-terrier mix who was terribly ill when he was brought to Deborah. Conventional medicine hadn't benefited him and Deborah didn't know what was wrong with him or how to help him. He had a lump on his back and she decided to consult with Milhouse to see whether to biopsy it.

He told Anita that he did not want to go through surgery. "Is there anything else you can do to help me?" he asked. He knew he had cancer and said that he was staying alive as long as he was in order to protect his people.

He requested that he not be kept at the hospital, he wanted to be allowed to go home after any treatment. He told Anita that there were some amino acids that would help him and he named a few specific ones. Deborah was quick to point out to me that Anita has no knowledge of the body's chemistry, but she reported the names he gave her and they were indeed amino acids. Milhouse was given the requested amino acids and they seemed to make him feel better. "He almost knew more about what was going on in his body, on a chemical basis, than any of us," Deborah says.

Milhouse lived another two weeks or so after that initial contact. Deborah had to go out of town during that time, and Milhouse's people called Anita in Deborah's absence when they felt it was time to let him go. The little dog requested that they wait until Deborah returned to town so that she could be the one to put him to sleep. They honored that request.

Susan Rifkin Ajamian turned to Dawn Hayman when her horses became mysteriously ill. She'd consulted various vets and still hadn't determined what exactly was wrong. With the primary veterinarian's blessing, they had a session with Dawn in which one of the horses described technical information, in detail. Neither Dawn nor Susan understood the information, but they dutifully took it down. The vet understood. They arranged a second consult and sent the transcript to the vet. In that session the horse described what was going on in his body at the cellular level. With this information, the vet was able to find a solution to the health problem.

For some clients of animal communicators, calling the communicator is like calling 911. When Roni Bailey came home and found her cat, Sydney, paralyzed, the first thing she did was to place calls to several animal communicators.

Roni didn't know how Sydney had been hurt and when she rushed her to the veterinarian, the vet assumed that the cat had swallowed antifreeze, which can be lethal. Not knowing for a fact whether this was true, but not willing to risk that it might be, the vet began administering the antidote, alcohol, to Sydney.

When Gail De Sciose returned Roni's call, Roni asked her to contact Sydney and see if she could find out what had happened. Sydney told her that that she hadn't eaten anything poisonous. Rather, Sydney sent Gail a picture of an unusual configuration of picnic tables: two picnic tables and two benches. Both benches were on one side of one table. That, in fact, was exactly the formation of picnic tables in Roni's backyard. Sydney showed Gail that she had injured herself jumping up to a picnic table from the ground.

Based on that information, Roni had the veterinarian stop the treatment for antifreeze poisoning. Sydney had to stay in the hospital for two weeks until she was stable enough to go home. Gail touched base with Sydney every day of her hospitalization. When the vet told

Roni that Sydney needed to eat, she asked Gail to communicate that to Sydney. The next day, Sydney began eating. The process was repeated for drinking.

When the vet told Roni that Sydney wouldn't have a chance of recovery unless she started moving soon, Gail told the cat that the doctors needed to see some sign of responsiveness. And she moved a little. "It seemed like every day there was something new that I told her through Gail to do. And every time, Gail obviously got through," says Roni. These incremental steps were vital for Sydney's recovery. "It was like climbing a ladder," says Roni. "It was incredible."

After nearly two weeks in the hospital, Sydney was strong enough not to need supportive care. But the veterinarian wanted to keep her at the hospital and run more diagnostic tests. Gail told Roni that Sydney didn't want the tests and instead wanted to go home. Since Roni was convinced that Sydney hadn't ingested poison, Roni, a veterinary technician, ignored the vet's advice and had her cat—who still couldn't walk—discharged. "I had to fight for the discharge," Roni recalls.

Once Roni got Sydney home, the real work began. Sydney required a lot of care, day in and day out, for six long weeks. Gail spoke with Sydney once a week during the home care. At the end of that six-week period, Sydney began to walk.

Roni remembers the day that Sydney first walked again. "I'll never forget it," she recalls. "It was exactly six weeks from the day I brought her home. I woke up in the morning and, to my surprise, Sydney wasn't on her bed in my room. She was in the kitchen standing at her bowl and eating. I believe to this day that she is walking because of what I did with Gail."

Six months later, Sydney moves just as fast as any cat. She is a little wobbly, which Roni attributes to damage from the antifreeze antidote. "Unfortunately, she was misdiagnosed," says Roni. If it weren't for Gail's help, the misdiagnosis might not have been discovered until after even more damage was done. "Without Gail, I probably would have gone through a lot of different treatments and tests that could have hurt my cat," says Roni.

Although the experience was traumatic for Sydney and for Roni, Gail's caring made it a positive episode in her life. "I really don't know what I would have done if I didn't know Gail. I am happy to have someone like her in my life."

As Gail's work with Sydney demonstrates, an animal communicator can be an emotional lifeline to an ailing animal. Gail recalls working with a once-feral cat named Timothy (he informed Gail of his name). While feral, Timothy had somehow mangled a leg but wouldn't allow himself to be handled by a veterinarian. His rescuer asked Gail to talk with him. After their talk, Timothy agreed to cooperate with the vet so that he could get well.

In addition to his injured leg (which eventually had to be amputated) Timothy tested positive for feline AIDS and had to be isolated at the animal hospital where he was staying. Gail spoke to him every day for 18 months, while he stayed at the animal hospital and during his transition to his new home.

Timothy ended up going to a "halfway house" for cats. Gail spoke with all the cats in the house before Timothy moved there and explained to them that it was imperative that they not fight with Timothy, since a bite could transmit his disease. She received assurances from the cats that they would not fight with him. The resident cats have kept their promise, and Timothy is now a happy housecat with full run of the house. Gail refers to him as her "poster child."

An animal communicator can help your animal tell you how he feels about proposed medical treatments. Some animals are gung-ho about a complex treatment, and willing to do anything to get well. Others, such as Milhouse, have distinct treatment preferences. By using the services of an animal communicator, you can discover your animal's wishes or reassure him about what needs to be done.

Judy Collins of Dallas, Texas, had a beloved parakeet named Raffi who had been diagnosed with a respiratory infection. When the illness did not respond to treatment, the vets wanted to x-ray the tiny bird, under general anesthesia, in order to find out if he had any "tumors, foreign objects or metal" inside of him. (The veterinary staff repeated the phrase several times.)

Judy asked Gail to talk with Raffi about the x-ray procedure. Gail asked Raffi if he knew what the nature of his health problem was. Raffi said, "I don't know what is wrong. But I know that I don't have any tumors, foreign objects or metal in me."

All Raffi knew was that there was terrible pressure in his throat and in his gut. "I'll do anything it takes to get better," he said. He told Judy to set up the x-ray and he'd do his part to get through it.

When Judy went to pick Raffi up at the vet's office after the x-rays, the vet commented that the little bird was a trooper. "He did exceptionally well under the anesthesia," he said. Judy knew that Raffi had kept his promise to do his part to make the procedure go well. The x-rays revealed that Raffi was not suffering from a respiratory infection but, rather, had a goiter.

TALKING TO ANIMALS TO EASE RECOVERY

Animal communicators can make an animal's recovery much easier. When Susan Rifkin Ajamian's horse, Richie, had to be operated on to have a tumor removed, the surgery was much more involved and lengthy than they'd anticipated. Anita Curtis and two of her students spoke with Richie before, during and after his surgery. They told him that when he woke up he would be on his side, and that it would be very important for him to stay on his side until he was strong enough to get up on his feet and stay up because struggling to get to his feet, then falling, could do serious damage. "Wait until you're strong enough," they told him. He received their message and was very careful about getting up.

For animals who are afraid of the vet, communicating with them—even if it's out loud and not through a professional—can help a great deal. Sherry Moore's Doberman Pinscher, Niko, underwent a battery of medical tests to try to get to the bottom of some of his aggressive behavior problems. Like many dogs, he became anxious at the vet's office and each visit became a battle.

"I wasn't aware that I needed to explain things to my dogs," says Moore. But after Patty Summers told her of the importance of keeping animals abreast of the developments in their lives, Sherry began giving Niko a running commentary about his upcoming vet visits. The night before the visit, and again in the car on the way to the office, Sherry would explain exactly what was going to happen and how it would make him feel. And Niko responded by behaving beautifully at the vet. "He takes stitches with only local anesthesia and no muzzle," says Moore, as long as she explains what's going on.

COMMUNICATORS AS HEALERS

Although animal communicators cannot ethically diagnose your animal, they can provide suggestions for some safe, healing treatments that you might seek through an alternative practitioner. The Code of Ethics of Interspecies Telepathic Communicators states in part: "We may also assist through handling of stresses, counseling, and other gentle healing methods. We let clients decide for themselves how to work with healing their animal companions' distress, disease or injury, given all the information available."

Gail De Sciose, who is a trained Reiki practitioner, keeps up-to-date with alternative medicine modalities. She helped her client Helen Koster obtain relief for her injured cat. One day Helen came home to find her very active cat, Annie, unable to jump. She couldn't even get up on the couch. Annie's condition worsened, to the point where she couldn't move her hind legs at all and had to drag herself by her front legs. Through Gail, Annie told Helen that she'd injured herself jumping off an armoire.

Annie's therapy and her slow, 18-month climb to recovery was aided immensely by Gail, says Helen. "Gail was Annie's therapist and coach." Helen sought all manner of alternative help for Annie, much of it suggested by Gail, including homeopathy, acupuncture and chiropractic. Gail would check with Annie regularly to see how she was feeling, and whether the current therapies were helping. Gail even accompanied Helen and Annie to a holistic veterinarian's office a few hours away.

Locating the Pain

Nancy Mueller was able to help Diane Beuthe ascertain that her horse had broken ribs. Nancy's husband Robert, who is a veterinary chiropractor, had been called in for an adjustment on the horse's spine because the horse was having problems being saddled. But the spinal adjustment didn't help. Nancy connected with the horse, then called Bob at the barn and suggested he try the fifth rib on the right side. Bob tried adjusting that rib. It was clear that he'd found the painful area and he was able to treat the problem. "We wouldn't have looked at the ribs if it weren't for Nancy," Diane says.

Dawn Hayman performed a similar service for Amy Nowak's mare Sophie. She was exhibiting some back pain and Amy had Dawn check with Sophie to see where she hurt. Dawn was able to pinpoint an area of the spine that was painful to Sophie. Amy had a well-known and well-respected chiropractor come to make an adjustment, but when he was finished, it was clear to Amy that he hadn't addressed the problem area; she could see no release of the pain on Sophie's part. So she asked him if he had adjusted the particular part of the spine that Dawn had suggested (she'd kept Dawn's suggestion to herself). "As a matter of fact, I didn't," he said. He examined that area and found that she was indeed out of alignment there. When he made the adjustment, Sophie displayed immediate relief.

With their long spines, back pain is not uncommon in horses. Cheryl Weeks' black gelding, Tate, was suffering from a sore back and bouts of lameness. All types of diagnostic tools and treatments were tried, but to no avail. Then Cheryl asked Dawn to speak with Tate. He told her that his back hurt because of his feet. No one had thought to look at Tate's feet! That information was brought to the veterinarian at the University of Pennsylvania's New Bolton Equine Center. The vet immediately saw that the angle of Tate's hooves was so far off, it was as if he were "walking on one high heel and one sneaker." This accounted for the back pain and lameness. Cheryl found a new farrier who straightened out the angles of Tate's feet and the pain vanished. Tate was all right again and the lameness became a thing of the past.

Cheryl's other horse, Jiggs, had a similar experience. She was lame with no apparent injury. Jiggs told Dawn that her right front foot was sore, on the right side. Cheryl's farrier is also Anita Curtis' farrier, and is accustomed to learning of problems straight from the horse's mouth. He pulled off Jigg's right front shoe to take a look and saw that, sure enough, he had come a little too close to the quick with a nail on the right side of her right front foot. Her shoe was reset and she was no longer lame.

Dawn also helped Cheryl get a very early diagnosis of arthritis for Jiggs. The horse had had a bone spur removed on her right front leg, and when Cheryl checked in with Jiggs (through Dawn) to make sure that it had healed well, Jiggs told Dawn that her right side felt fine, but that her left rear leg hurt. They had her x-rayed and found that she was developing arthritis in that leg.

Emotional Origins for Health Concerns

As Dawn Hayman has pointed out, many behavioral problems are physical in origin. For example, a sound-sensitive animal who lashes out at a loud noise might be suffering from a cervical disc misalignment that amplifies sound. Or a dog who is in pain may bite when someone approaches for fear that the person will cause more pain.

Similarly, health problems can be emotional in origin. And an animal communicator can help you understand (and perhaps alleviate) the emotional disturbance. When Lisa Papp's cat Taffy was suffering the injustices of living with Tinker, a cat he didn't like (one whose pastime was harassing Taffy), he became physically ill. He became lethargic: Gail De Sciose told Lisa that Taffy had no energy in his legs. As soon as Gail helped the Papps understand that everyone concerned would be better off if Tinker were found a new home, Taffy's health almost instantly improved.

Dawn Hayman worked with a pony who had stopped eating after she'd been moved to a different barn. The pony's person didn't move him from the barn where he was living until a year after she'd acquired him. She asked Dawn to find out why, after the move, the pony wouldn't eat.

The pony told Dawn that he was deeply grieving for another pony who used to live with him at the first barn. "He will never find me," he said. He described to Dawn that as long as he was at his original barn, his best friend might come back to join him. But now that he had moved, there was no hope for his friend to find him.

Dawn's client looked into the situation and discovered, by odd coincidence, that the two ponies now lived only five miles apart from one another. She trucked her pony over to see his old friend. "It was the most joyous reunion you could imagine," says Dawn. The two friends now get together once a month to run and play together.

Flower Essences Used in Conjunction with Animal Communication

Eighty-five percent of Sharon Callahan's clients come through referrals from veterinarians. Holistic vets, in particular, seem to appreciate her expertise in flower remedy therapy, as well as her animal communication skills. Sharon Callahan has developed a line of flower essences, made from the wildflowers that grow near her home at the base of Mount Shasta. These essences, developed specifically for animals and sold under the name Anaflora, are an integral part of her animal communication work. The essences are liquid preparations used to address emotional issues. They are made from the blossoms of flowering plants.

According to the Anaflora brochure, Sharon's essences are "potent non-aromatic vibrational liquids that are taken internally to create profound healing and change. They get quickly to the heart of the issue, creating balance, well-being and health."

The communication session that Sharon has with a client helps pinpoint the specific essence that will help the animal (though Sharon also uses her intuition to select essences from among the more than 120 formulations that she has created). In turn, the essence helps complete the emotional healing that the animal communication session begins. Sharon says that the animal communication helps identify the emotions that need to be addressed with flower essences. "So often we misinterpret our animals' emotions," she says. "When you ask them themselves it helps."

Sharon will frequently suggest that both human and animal take the same essence. "I find that there is so much emotional transference between human and animal companions that if we don't address the human's emotions, we don't address the animal's," she says. When both human and animal companions take the same flower essences, a healing resonance is created, she says. This "serves as a gesture of cooperation which greatly facilitates the healing process."

Sharon is not alone in her promotion of flower essences. Many other animal communicators recommend their use. It is not unusual for animals to have emotional problems, and flower essences can be important tools in helping animals stabilize their emotions.

Susan Goldstein, along with her husband veterinarian Bob Goldstein, owns Earth Animals, a holistic wellness center in Westport, Connecticut, which is comprised of a telephone-consult service, retail store and publishing enterprise. Animal communication is an integral part of their phone practice. "We would be clinically remiss if we didn't focus on the emotions of our patients," says Susan. Toward that end, the Goldsteins keep Sharon Callahan on staff as a full-time animal communicator. They also refer clients to Gail De Sciose. Susan herself is able to communicate telepathically with her own animals, but she says she doesn't have enough confidence in her abilities to do it for others.

Susan's commitment to the emotional aspects of animals—as ascertained by telepathic animal communication—is complete. "In 2000 there won't be a patient that goes through this clinic that isn't checked on emotionally and spiritually," she declared in late 1999.

"I am convinced that there has to be an emotional weakness, something that is out of balance, in order for the body to be diseased. A lot of times a communicator will be able to offset the healing and work in adjunct with our nutritional remedies." Just the fact that the animal is heard and has a chance to share the experience that has manifested itself in its body can help heal," she says.

TAKING AN ANIMAL'S SUGGESTIONS TO HEART

When consulted, animals will occasionally have suggestions to make for their treatment plan. Milhouse recommended amino acids. My Standard Poodle, Scout, recommended that her brother, Kramer, go to the chiropractor.

I had begun taking Scout to a gentle, soft-spoken veterinary chiropractor, named Robert Mueller (husband of animal communicator Nancy Mueller), to help mitigate some structural problems she'd suffered after a fall she'd taken while chasing Kramer in the snow. In a session with Ginny Debbink, I asked Scout how she was feeling and she said she felt pretty good, "but not as good as I feel after seeing The Soft Man."

Out of the blue, she suggested that Kramer be taken to the chiropractor as well. The thought hadn't occurred to me. When I asked her why, she said, "I think it would help his overall health." (Kramer suffers from autoimmune disease brought on by overvaccination.) "Besides," she added, "everyone's out of alignment."

I checked with Kramer's homeopathic veterinarian who gave me the green light to take him to the chiropractor. Sure enough, Scout was right. Kramer had a number of vertebrae out of alignment. He seemed to enjoy the adjustment a fact he confirmed when I spoke with him through Gail De Sciose. I'm proud to say that I take medical advice from my dog!

Chapter 9

Animals Can Help Decide When to Let Go

The decision about whether to euthanize a beloved animal is one of the most agonizing decisions an animal lover can make. Animal communicators can help by connecting with the animal and discussing whether he or she is ready to go.

This function of an animal communicator is the one that Diane Beuthe, a client of Nancy Mueller, values the most. "I like to think that animals should die with the dignity they lived with," Diane says. "An animal communicator can take any doubt out of your mind that you are doing the right thing."

Diane tells the story of her horse, Mac, a quarter horse who was actively used in fox hunting. When Mac became ill and cancer was discovered, he told Diane (through Nancy) that he was ready to go immediately. If he couldn't hunt, he wasn't interested in continuing to live. Unfortunately, it wasn't possible for him to be euthanized immediately because it was Easter week and Diane's grandchildren were visiting. Moreover, the heavy excavation equipment needed to dig a grave for him at their farm wasn't available. Mac was very disappointed that he would have to wait a week.

But the children went home early and the equipment miraculously became available, so Nancy told Mac that he would be released the next day, a Thursday. Diane says that all day, Mac stood at the gate and watched every move that Diane and her husband made. Diane felt he was telling them, "Come on, it's Thursday!" When Nancy's husband, Bob, a veterinarian arrived to put Mac down, the horse dropped to the ground before the lethal dose was completed. "His heart stopped immediately," says Diane. He was more than ready to go. "Knowing that he really wanted out of this life really helped," says Diane.

Working with clients whose animals are dying is one of the most rewarding aspects of her work, says Anita Curtis. She enjoys putting people's mind at ease by letting them know that their animal friend is ready to pass on and that the animal is not afraid. Sometimes she can relay special requests that help both the person and the animal feel better. "They might want to be buried in a yellow blanket, for example," she explains.

Anita also helps people by letting them know if their animal says he'll visit from the spirit world. An animal might say, "I'll be back to comfort you," and describe a room in the house. The person can then go to that room, close their eyes and ask the animal to come to them.

ANIMALS DON'T FEAR DEATH

Time and again, communicators have told me that animals don't share the fear of death that humans harbor. "They understand the cycle of the universe and know that death is the beginning of a new cycle," says Nancy Mueller.

"I have not had an animal yet who was afraid of dying, once it was explained to them," says Patty Summers. Many animal companions seem to be more afraid of hurting their people by dying than the actual death itself. "Animals tend to hang on for the people, not for themselves," says Gail De Sciose.

Cathy Barash could tell that her beloved orange tabby cat, Sebastian, was not doing well. Sebastian, 14 years old and living with cancer, had stopped eating. He grew weaker and thinner, but he wasn't acting sick and did not seem to be in any pain. Barash worked from home for two weeks, determined to spend as much high-quality time with Sebastian as she could give him. They enjoyed snuggling in the sun and long talks. During that time, Cathy told him that it's okay to let go of his frail body, but he didn't seem to be ready yet. She contacted Gail De Sciose to confirm that Sebastian wasn't in pain and didn't want to be put to sleep.

Gail related to Cathy the sensations she felt in her own body, indicating how Sebastian was feeling. When Cathy relayed that information to her veterinarian, he confirmed that it was exactly what he would expect Sebastian to feel, based on his illness. Sebastian told Cathy that he knew he was nearing the end of his time but that he wanted "to see a couple more sunny days." He confirmed that he wasn't in any pain, and that he didn't want any assistance, other than Cathy's company, in dying.

Despite his refusal of food, Sebastian remained agile, jumping onto the table and going outside rather than using his litterbox. Cathy was certain that, even as he grew weaker, he was in no hurry to exit this world.

Gail's communication with Sebastian helped Cathy immensely. "It was reassuring to know that he wanted the same thing as I did, to be able to die naturally and have me with him when he made the transition," says Cathy. Ten days after that communication, Sebastian died in Cathy's arms. He had stopped eating 16 days earlier.

SAYING GOODBYE

When Margo Mildvan's Keeshond, Keesha, was diagnosed with lung cancer, she turned to Ginny Debbink to see how Keesha was really feeling. Keesha told Ginny that she knew she was sick, and that her illness was deadly, but that she wasn't ready to go—she had a lot more to teach Margo before she passed on. "I think she was here to teach me about life," says Margo. "She taught me not to let the little things get to me." Keesha lived for a year after her diagnosis. During that last year, she continued to help Margo understand what was important in life. "I would open the door, and if she had any inkling she might be going for a ride she would bound out to the car," recalls Margo. "She was dying, but her attitude seemed to be, 'I can't fix this, but I can enjoy life.'"

Margo also asked Ginny to touch base with her other dogs, Apollo and Roxy, to make sure that they understood about Keesha's illness. Naturally, they did. And they didn't resent the extra attention that Keesha required from her mom and dad. Apollo told Margo, "It's okay. I understand that this is where your energy needs to be. I understand you need time with Keesha. I just want a little more playtime."

As Keesha's illness progressed and the end seemed closer, Margo dreaded having to put Keesha to sleep. One day in July 1999, she came home to find that Keesha had lost control of her bodily functions. As she gently bathed her, she knew this was the end. "Inside of this dog's body was a spirit that could go on forever," says Margo. "But the body was failing and I was terrified."

Margo called Ginny, who made an immediate connection with Keesha. Ginny asked the sick dog whether she felt it was time. Her response, Margo recalls, was "We are in the window. It is okay [for me to go now], but I could go a lot longer if you want me to, even though there will be a lot of pain." Keesha told Ginny that what she really wanted was to be cleaned up and look pretty.

Margo called the veterinarian and arranged for a house call the next day in order for Keesha to be euthanized at home. "That evening was the most peaceful time," recalls Margo. "We just hung out outside and did what Keesha wanted to do."

The next day, Margo spoke out loud to Apollo and Roxy, and told them exactly what was going to transpire. When the vet drove up the Mildvan's long driveway, Apollo, the self-appointed watch dog who always alerts when a car approaches, sat at the window and didn't utter a sound. "I'm sure he knew exactly who it was and he didn't want to raise a ruckus," says Margo.

Keesha left this life, at home, in Margo's arms that afternoon. "It was the most peaceful feeling afterward," she says. "I couldn't have done it without Ginny, without making sure that Keesha was okay with it." Margo knew intellectually that it was time, but she had too much respect for Keesha not to ask for her permission beforehand.

UNDERSTANDING FINAL REQUESTS

An animal communicator can relay an animal's wishes about how he wants to die, and these wishes can be very specific. Sebastian didn't want to be euthanized, for example. Deborah Mack, a holistic veterinarian, recommends to those clients she feels would be open to it that they consult an animal communicator and ask their dying animal whether it is time for them to go. "It takes the question [of whether they're doing the right thing] out of their mind," she says.

When her own dog, Jazz, was ill, Deborah asked Anita Curtis to talk with the English Setter about her impending death. Jazz wanted to try to go on her own, she said, but knew that if she needed help, Deborah would know. Jazz specifically requested that Deborah not be the one to euthanize her, so that she could be in Deborah's arms at the end. She requested that Deborah's associate be the one to administer the final injection. Jazz made a good choice, says Deborah. "I couldn't have taken part in the emotional aspect if I were acting as a veterinarian," she says. "I got to be where I was supposed to be, which was holding her."

When one animal in a family is ill and dying, the other animals in the household are affected. Including the other animals in any communication you have about the ill animal can help them with the passing, too.

During the communication session in which they consulted Jazz about her passing, Anita also spoke with Jazz's son, Gator. He wanted to know if there was anything that he could do to help, or would he just get in the way. Anita and Deborah assured him that anything he could do to help would be welcome.

"From that point on, Gator felt free to take care of Jazz," recalls Deborah. He cleaned up after her, groomed her and was there for the euthanasia.

Animals tend to adjust to the death of their animal friends more easily than humans, say animal communicators. "Animals release trauma very quickly," says Gail De Sciose. "They don't need years of therapy like humans."

If one of your animal friends dies (or a human family member, for that matter), your surviving animal will doubtless miss him. But he's worried about you, too. "Sometimes we think the animal is in mourning, but they might be in pain for the human survivor," says Patty Summers. As you heal, so too will your animal.

PARTING INSIGHTS

Communicating with your ill animal can not only help reassure you that he's ready to leave his body, but also give your animal a chance to share his parting insights with you. Helen Koster, a client of Gail De Sciose, spoke with her cat, Lillian, through Gail the night before she was euthanized after suffering from mouth cancer. Gail had spoken to Lillian, who was a very frightened cat, many times.

Gail, who lives near Helen, went to Helen's apartment the night before Lillian's last veterinary appointment. "It was a very spiritual experience," says Helen. Helen asked Lillian if she wanted to pass away right there in her lap, but Lillian said that she didn't want to lose control of her bodily functions in Helen's lap. She did say that she was ready to go, which made her passing at the vet's office the next day much easier.

That last night, Lillian left Helen with some profound sentiments. "I've chosen to live my life in a very restricted and narrow way due to my fears," she said to Gail. "Please tell Helen not to restrict herself in any way. She must follow where her heart tells her to go and she must not look backward on anything which is not in that quest."

When Gail asked Lillian if she were ready to make the transition into the spirit world, Lillian said, "I am complete now that I have said my goodbyes. There is nothing more I can do in this body as Lillian. I just need to move on."

Helen was deeply moved by Lillian's message to her. "Lillian taught me not to ever let my fears restrict me," she says. "Gail was such a big part of making Lillian's passing beautiful."

There are those who, even when they hear directly from their animal friend that he's ready to pass away, can't accept it. That's human nature. Cheryl Weeks, who is able to communicate telepathically with her own animals, recalls that when her first Australian Shepherd, Tasha, suddenly became ill, Cheryl wasn't ready to let her go. Tasha was feeling poorly and was passing blood, but the veterinarian didn't know what was wrong with her and prescribed some medication for the bleeding. The next day when Cheryl came home from work, Tasha clearly (and loudly) told Cheryl, "I'm dying." Cheryl argued with her, "No, you're not dying, the doctor gave you medication; you're going to eat and get well and be fine. I don't want to hear you're dying." Tasha stopped arguing, but the next day when Cheryl returned home from work she found that Tasha was in a coma; Cheryl had to have her put down. "I have always felt guilty for not accepting her diagnosis and arguing with her, but have always been grateful to her for teaching me that animals very clearly can communicate if you choose to listen," says Cheryl.

Chapter 10

Communicating with Departed Animals

··

How you feel about what happens after a being dies is deeply rooted in your personal belief systems and religion. The animal communicators I interviewed for this book seemed to share a common belief that after a being has died (or "left his body" or "entered the spirit world"), it is only his physical body that is gone. His spirit lives on. "Death is not an ending," says Patty Summers. "The physical body is just a vessel."

This is a comforting belief for those who would like to talk with their animals after they've passed away. Since telepathic communication doesn't take place on the physical plane, talking with departed animals works on the same principles of telepathic connection as talking with living ones. A departed animal connects with a communicator just like a living one does. "You always have a heart connection with your animals whether or not they are still living," says Dawn Hayman.

The communicators I spoke with say that having the opportunity to talk with their departed animal friends provides a great comfort to their clients. "It brings a lot of peace to let them know that their animals are okay," says Patty Summers.

As open as she was to communicating with living animals, Gail De Sciose once had her doubts about speaking with those who had passed on. "I was skeptical," she remembers, "but an animal showed me." At the time, Gail was volunteering at the ASPCA. There, she met a Sheltie who was ailing. Gail knew that that the dog was going to be euthanized between Gail's weekend visits. In the middle of the week, the Sheltie sent her an image of herself running and happy. "She actually came to me and showed me that she was okay." That experience showed Gail that she could, in fact, communicate with departed animals. She's very grateful to that Sheltie. "I never even knew her name, but she was a sweetie," she says.

Ninety-nine percent of the deceased animals who Dawn Hayman contacts want their people to know that they still feel connected to them and that every time the person thinks of them, they feel it. "They always make it the first thing that they say," says Dawn.

Even after death, some animals carry on the roles they had in life, something that their people can confirm through animal communication. When she was alive, Lindy Sanford's English Setter, Patience, was the ultimate mother. She looked after all the puppies in the family, and even helped raise some orphaned calves on their farm. "She'd lick them by the hour. And she'd stand outside their stall and scold them when they did something she didn't want," Lindy recalls. "Even when the calves had grown into cows, she would check in on them."

Shortly after her death, Patience told Lindy (through animal communicator Becky Blanton), that she wanted Lindy to feed her body to the kittens that Patience had seen on the farm during her morning walkabout on the farm's fenced six acres. Lindy didn't know about any kittens out on the farm, but she went to the spot that Patience had described and found a litter of fox kits. The ultimate mother, Patience wanted her body left there for the fox kits to feed on. Lindy couldn't bring herself to allow Patience's body to be devoured, so she had her cremated and instead regularly fed the fox kits as they grew up. Lindy says that if it weren't for Patience, she never would have known about the little foxes who needed her help. "They're fine now, and have gone on with their lives," she says.

Lindy still feels Patience's presence and believes that she's still keeping a close eye on the puppies. "Her job is to watch these puppies we have now and make sure they are all right," she says.

Viola Cruz is blind and uses a guide dog from Guide Dogs for the Blind. She was extremely close to her first guide dog, Cochise. "He couldn't have been a more perfect first dog," Viola says. Cochise, a Golden Retriever, worked with Viola for twelve years and continued living with her after he was retired because he was going deaf. He died at the age of 14.

Several years after he died, Viola spoke with Cochise through Ginny Debbink. "I wanted to contact him and tell him that I still love him and miss him. He said he knew." Viola felt Cochise's presence when she got her third guide dog, Alberta. Viola had had some difficulty with her second guide dog and retired him at an early age. Cochise said that he wanted to make sure that Alberta was going to be a good fit. "He was worried about me, but knew I was going to be okay. I promised him that we'd make it work out."

The last time that Viola spoke with Cochise, he said that he was going to help someone else. "This upset me more than I could tell him," says Viola, who had felt Cochise's healing presence in the past but no longer senses that he is still with her.

Amy Nowak's mare, Sophie, died nine years ago. When she was still alive, Amy spoke with her through Dawn Hayman on a regular basis. This situation didn't change after Sophie became ill and died at the age of 17. Amy uses Dawn's services every six weeks and each time she talks to her animals through Dawn, she makes sure to check in with Sophie. It's clear that the relationship between Amy and Sophie wasn't altered by Sophie's death. "She's so funny," says Amy. "She says that she is in heaven, where it is sunny and there is lots of grass but no flies."

Amy and Sophie talk about Sophie coming back in another body. Amy tries to press her and find out when she'll be back. Sophie says she knows she will come back to Amy but she doesn't know when; she is resting.

DISCOVERING REINCARNATION THROUGH COMMUNICATION

Lindy Sanford's dog Clare was hit by a car and died when she was only nine months old. Lindy was out of town tending her dying mother when Clare was killed. A little over one year later, another puppy, Miss Clairol, was born to Clare's parents. Lindy is convinced that Clare has come back as Clairol. After communicating with Clairol, Patty confirmed it. By coming back, Clare gave Lindy a special gift: She helped her cope with the loss of her own mother. "Clare taught me that I could make it through my mother's death because we all come back. I'll see my mother again," Lindy says with conviction.

Clare is not the only animal in Lindy's life to return to her. Lindy had a mare named Shadow who was in the barn nursing her five-month-old chestnut foal when she was struck by lightning. Both the mare and foal were killed and the barn burned to the ground.

Some months later, a new foal was born. This filly looked exactly like Shadow and Lindy thought that she had come back in the form of the new foal. But the new mare's personality—she was an angry horse—was different from Shadow's. Patty spoke with her and learned that Lindy had misidentified her. "I see her as a chestnut foal," said Patty. The horse had come back looking identical to the mother, but with the spirit of the colt. Once she was recognized for who she really was, the horse's anger dissipated. "She was so angry at not having been given a chance to live, but she was able to let that go," says Lindy. "We don't talk about her old life."

Like Lindy Sanford, Deborah Mack, D.V.M., breeds English Setters. Deborah is still learning from her departed English Setter, Jazz. "She was my teacher. She had a tremendous amount of wisdom." Jazz told Deborah (through Anita Curtis) that it was time for her to go, so that she could continue to teach Deborah. "She told me, 'Where you are at in your spiritual journey, you are having a hard time learning to trust what you don't see. For you to progress in your practice, you have to trust. The only way I can continue to be your teacher is in a spiritual form,'" says Deborah. "So she has chosen not to come back; she is still teaching."

Jazz watches over the puppies. She helped Deborah select a puppy from a litter that Deborah wasn't able to visit. "She told me to take the tri-colored female. And she was right."

Jazz's son, Gator, by contrast, has already come back, just over a year after he passed away. When Gator became ill, Deborah asked him to come back to her in a healthy body. He returned in a litter that Deborah bred. Deborah asked Gator to give her a sign and let her know which puppy (of the nine in the litter) he had come back as. She assumed he would pick a big-boned male, since he had been very large and beautiful (and very vain) the first time around.

All the puppies were born white. But one of the puppies had a brown spot under his ear just like Gator had. She spied the spot as she delivered the puppy. "I knew the moment I touched this puppy that it was him." Sure enough, this puppy grew up to be strong and inquisitive, just like Gator was. He already seemed to know the house, leaving his littermates to make a beeline for the kitchen the first time they managed to escape the whelping box, at the age of four weeks. Anita confirmed that the new puppy, Shobi, was indeed Gator reincarnated. "But I knew that before," says Deborah. In a prior communication, Gator told Deborah, "My mother is your spiritual teacher and I am your physical support."

A client of Gail De Sciose, Katherine Roberts, has a new puppy, an Icelandic Sheepdog named Daphne. Daphne was named after the first Golden Retriever that Katherine and her husband lived with after they were married. That precious dog passed away four years ago and Katherine's husband Mark felt she would come back as an Icelandic Sheepdog, a breed they'd become intrigued by when they got involved with Icelandic horses. Mark had casually mentioned to friends in Iceland that they were interested in the breed (there are only 250 Icelandic Sheepdogs in Iceland and very few in the United States). Those friends took that as a request to find a puppy and soon after, the Roberts received a call that their puppy was on the way.

"As soon as we met her at the airport we knew it was Daphne come back," says Katherine. "I opened her crate and she came into my arms and started snuggling. She sleeps in the same spot, and does all the same things that the first Daphne did."

Sharing a Body?

Patti Limber had a ferret called Shadow (named for the way he followed her wherever she went). Shadow was Patti's soul mate. When he became ill, Patti sought out an animal communicator at a psychic fair to talk with him. She learned that his medication made him feel worse, so she took that information to the veterinarian and had his medication changed. She also tried some homeopathic medicine and flower essences at the suggestion of Rachel Perzanowski, the communicator. Both seemed to help, but eventually Shadow became sicker and told Patti he was ready to make the transition out of this life.

A month after he died, Patti asked Rachel to check in on him. He told Patti that he would return to her within one year in the form of a dog or a ferret.

Five months after Shadow's death, Patti took in a homeless ferret she named Tyler. She was amazed that Tyler fit in with her other ferrets very easily. "The others sniffed him and went right along and played with him as though they knew him." Such behavior is highly unusual for ferrets, says Patti.

As Tyler became healthier and put on more weight, he began resembling Shadow, particularly in his facial markings. One day, he came over to Patti's feet and lay on his back with his feet up in the air. "I was blown away," said Patti. "Only Shadow did that and it meant 'attention, please.'" She wondered if Shadow had returned.

She consulted Rachel once again and asked her to talk with Tyler. Rachel was surprised by what she heard when she connected with him. She heard two voices: one was Tyler and one was Shadow. Shadow said that Tyler was in charge of the physical and he was in charge of the spiritual. "It strongly appears that we have some sort of blending of souls," says Patti. "Somehow Shadow 'hopped a ride' [with Tyler] to return to me." She and Rachel are searching for someone with more experience in this type of event to explain the occurrence.

Identifying Returned Animals

For communicator Anita Curtis, one of the more rewarding aspects of her work is helping people identify reincarnated animals. The animal will usually give his person a clue, she says. "I'll come back when the weather is really hot." Or "Look for me on a farm." Clients will call her and ask her to find out the form that their animal has come back in. "They come back in a package that is going to be attractive to the person," she says.

How can you recognize that your new animal is your old animal in a different form? "When they show up, they walk in the house like they know where they are," says Anita. "There is a look that you recognize. They take on certain characteristics." Anita says it's important to remember that your new animal is not a replacement, but rather a continuance.

Anita's own dog came back to her. "He came in and I knew who he was." Anita hadn't had a dog in five years. When he arrived home, the new dog went out in the backyard. "He began digging and unearthed a long-buried tennis ball," recalls Anita. "He said, 'Yep, it's still here.'" That dog, who was a female in her earlier incarnation, came back as a male. When Anita asked why, he said, "You were prejudiced."

Gail De Sciose had a client, living in Germany, who was devastated by the loss of her cat, Moritz, after he was attacked and killed by a dog. Gail contacted the cat, who said that he would be coming back as an orange tabby cat. Her client kept her eye out for an orange cat, but they are very rare in Germany. During a vacation in Italy, however, an orange and white kitten walked right up to the woman and stared at her. The client called Gail immediately from Italy to ask her to ascertain whether this cat was actually Moritz. Gail contacted Moritz, who stated grandly, "It is I, Moritz, and I am returned." The client brought the kitten back with her to Germany where he now lives happily with her.

Some animals say they need to rest before coming back, while others are anxious to return. Amy Nowak's horse, Sophie, is still resting after nine years. But Deborah Mack's dog, Gator, came back only a year after he passed away.

Sebastian, Cathy Barash's cat, whose passing was aided by Gail De Sciose, told Cathy before he died that he would be back, as another cat, after two winters had passed since his death. This has provided great comfort to Cathy, who eagerly awaits his return.

When Tania Smothers and her husband purchased a house, they were surprised to find a dog chained to a tree in the front yard. Being animal lovers, they adopted the dog, named Gigi, a 13-year-old shepherd mix with heartworm disease. They treated her for the heartworm, and Gigi was their devoted companion for two more years.

After Gigi died, Tania would see glimpses of a dog, out of the corner of her eye, when she'd look out the window. She suspected that she might be seeing Gigi's spirit, and when she spoke with Liz Anderson, an animal communicator, she confirmed that that was the case. Three years after she died, Gigi was still patrolling the family's acreage as she did when she was alive.

Gigi told the animal communicator that she wanted to come back to Tania. Early in 1999, Tania decided to act on her desire to have a Border Collie. She found a breeder and went to examine the litter of eight male puppies. As she picked each one up to try to make a choice, one of them clearly said to her, "Take me home, take me home." So clear was that message that Tania gave the puppy Take Me Home as his registered name. The puppy (whose call name is Crash) is Gigi reincarnated, Tania is certain.

"I truly believe it is her. I haven't seen her spirit any more." Little Crash worships the ground Tania walks on, she says, and had absolutely no adjustment period when she brought him home at the age of seven weeks. Crash excels in every way, Tania says. She made an effort to socialize him and bring him up right, but she thinks a large part of his good nature is Gigi. "I can look into his soul through his eyes," says Tania. "I have no doubt he is Gigi."

Walk-ins

On occasion, an animal will return as an adult animal, rather than being born. Communicators refer to this phenomenon as a "walk-in." "Walk-ins really spooked me at first," says Anita Curtis. "But I'm getting it firsthand from the animals and I keep getting it." Sometimes, Anita explains, an animal wants to come back very quickly and will trade places with an abandoned animal who has had a difficult life and wants to move on.

THE CONNECTION CONTINUES

Animal lovers know how deeply bound they feel to their animal companions. By communicating with our departed friends, we can maintain our connections with them, renewing the joy that they brought us and alleviating the pain of their passing.

Chapter 11

Finding Lost Animals

Finding lost animals seems like it would be one of the most logical applications of animal communication. If it doesn't matter where the animal is for a connection to be made, surely a communicator can contact a missing one. And once contacted, the lost animal can just tell her where he is, right? Then the humans could go pick him up and the problem is solved.

If only it were that simple.

Missing-animal work is one of the most difficult tasks that animal communicators are asked to do. "It's the thing I like to do the least," says Anita Curtis, who is one of the relatively few communicators who offer the service. "There is so much pain. Sometimes there is no closure, which is when it gets me."

Many animal communicators do not consent to doing the work (with occasional exceptions for established clients), not because they're not able to do it, but because it is so gut-wrenching. "It is emotionally exhausting," says Ginny Debbink. "It is very demanding work on a very deep level."

Missing-animal work can be difficult work at which to succeed; the lost animal might be confused and frightened. "It is their fear that gets them lost," says Ginny. "They don't have the presence of mind to figure out how to get home." Ginny tries to calm the animal and relate to him how important it is for his person that he get his bearings and try to come home.

Animal communicators can explain to dogs who have tags on their collars what the tag is for and encourage them to come out in the open and approach a person so the tag can be read, says Dawn Hayman. Most dogs become scared and go into hiding, rendering their identification tags useless.

Animals don't read, so they don't look up at street signs. An animal communicator looks through the animal's eyes, so she's getting an animal's perspective of the world, which is quite different from a human's point of view. "That's the hardest thing," says Alice McClure.

But just being able to see and describe surroundings doesn't mean that a communicator will be able to pinpoint the location. "It is unusual to be able to get enough information to help a person find the animal," says Sharon Callahan.

Sharon likes to use the example of a cat who is locked in a garage. If a communicator sees the cat's surroundings through the cat's eyes, what's she going to see? Some car tires, maybe some junk. The inside of one garage looks like the inside of lots of garages. And if the garage door is closed so no one can see in from the outside, it doesn't really matter what the inside looks like.

Sharon did once help locate a valuable Abyssinian cat, an indoor-only cat who was pregnant and due to deliver soon. She had slipped out of the house and her people were frantic, since she'd had difficulties delivering kittens in the past, and the thought of her trying to deliver kittens outside without them was terrifying.

Sharon was able to ascertain that the cat was hiding under a porch. She described what the cat saw from her hiding place, including a bike and some toys. She could also tell that the cat had gone down her driveway, turned left, and not walked too far (Sharon explains that sometimes she sees scenes like this from an aerial perspective). The cat's human companion went out on a search and saw the bike and toys in a yard a few blocks away. She looked under the porch and found her cat.

In addition to the difficulty of not being able to pinpoint a location, animal communicators are occasionally faced with the reality that the animal has left on his own accord and doesn't want to be found. That's a hard message to deliver and an even harder one to accept. "I find that animals are very seldom lost," says Sharon. "More often than not, they are exactly where they want to be."

Amy Heggie was faced with a such a message when her cat, Al, disappeared. He left the house and didn't come back just one week after one of her dogs, Tyler, had died. Al and Tyler had been inseparable. Ten days after Al left, Amy contacted Ginny Debbink and asked her to see if she could locate Al. What Ginny learned surprised Amy.

Al told Ginny that Tyler's death had left him lost and that he needed to "find out who Al was." So he left on a vision quest. "He'll come home if he can, but he's not sure if he's supposed to yet," says Amy. Al told Ginny that he loves Amy and one of her other dogs, Whisky, and wants to come home when the time is right.

The conversation with Ginny allayed Amy's worry that Al felt that Amy had killed Tyler. (Amy had taken him to be euthanized because he was very old and ill.) Al told Ginny that both he and Tyler trusted Amy to make the right decision and that he knew that Tyler's time was running down. "That part made me feel better," says Amy, "but the fact that he's staying gone out of choice is a little hard to deal with."

As hard as that news was to hear, Amy was glad to get the information. "He's a canny little guy and I have to have faith in his choices. I just miss him!" Ginny has checked in on Al and reported that his life force is still strong and that he's still searching. He'll come home when he's able and until that time Amy will just have to comfort herself with the knowledge that he's safe.

SUCCESS STORIES

Fortunately, there are many other cases with happier endings. Dawn Hayman does missing-animal work, despite the fact that she'd rather not. It's harder than other kinds of communication, she says, because when an animal is missing, their people tend to feel disconnected from the animal, which makes it harder for Dawn to connect with the lost animal. But every time she vows not to do it again, she has a success with a lost-animal case, to the delight of the client. And that motivates her to keep going, since she knows she's providing a valuable service.

Once such success was a lost Husky who had been missing for ten days before his owners contacted Dawn. A tree had fallen in their yard in New Jersey, breaking the fence, and the dog escaped. Huskies can cover a lot of territory in a short period of time, and Dawn was afraid that by the time she was on the case that the dog was far, far away.

The husband was highly skeptical of Dawn's skills and demanded specific information. Dawn told the couple that she would try to see the surroundings through the dog's eyes. "I had this preconceived notion of New Jersey being nothing but concrete," says Dawn. "But the dog told me he was in a wilderness area, near a river, and told me about all the wildlife." Apparently the dog was catching rabbits and chasing deer, but he was afraid of bears. Dawn was afraid of fueling the husband's skepticism, so she didn't even mention the bears to the couple—it didn't seem possible to her that the dog was seeing bears in New Jersey.

The dog said he'd been hanging around the same area for about a week. Dawn asked him if he could hear anything special. He said he heard a constant motor with a thumping sound coming from a green building with a chain link fence.

When Dawn related this to the couple, the woman said, "You know, dear, that sounds like that place near where we saw the bear in the river." Dawn was shocked because she hadn't mentioned any bear.

That location was about nine miles away from the couple's home and covered hundreds of acres. But they decided to look. The couple drove to the wilderness area and, even though it was after dark, they found the green building with the fence. They called their dog's name and all of a sudden he came running out of the woods and jumped in the car. When they returned home, they called Dawn. "Never once did I doubt your skills," said the husband.

Ginny Debbink had a client whose cat, Dottie, came up missing right after they moved. The client believed that the movers had accidentally let Dottie out. When Ginny connected with the cat, Dottie said that she was home and that she was in a safe, warm place. She said, "Don't worry, I'll be back when I'm ready."

Three days later, Dottie's people heard her meowing from inside a garment box in a closet. She had sought refuge from the disruption of the move and called for assistance only when she was ready.

Stacey Vornbrock's cat, Louis, slipped out of the house while under the care of a pet sitter. Stacy was out of town and was frantic when she received a phone call from the sitter saying that Louis had been missing for 24 hours.

A longtime friend of Sonya Fitzpatrick, Stacey called Sonya immediately. Sonya was able to connect with Louis and learn that he was still in the neighborhood. He said he could hear the cat sitter and Stacey's friend calling for him, but he was angry that the cat sitter hadn't looked very hard for him and vowed not to come home until Stacey returned. Sonya explained to Stacey that it's difficult to wander the neighborhood and find a lost cat. Because cats hide so easily, humans really have to rely on the cat to come home on his own.

Sonya stayed in touch with Louis, encouraging him to come home or (at least) not to wander far. She told him when Stacey was on her way home (yet another 24 hours later) and to Stacey's delight, Louis was there to greet her upon her return. "I absolutely attribute the fact that he came home to Sonya," she says.

CLOSURE

Communicators can help provide a sense of closure when an animal is missing. Marilyn Lorenzen turned to Sharon Callahan when her daughter's dog was stolen. Sharon was able to connect with the dog, who told her that he was happy in his new home. That may have been difficult to accept, but at least they knew that their dog was happy and safe.

Sometimes a missing animal has died. In that case, the communicator can still connect with the animal, but it can be difficult to tell whether the animal is dead or alive because the animal's spirit remains the same whether or not the animal is living in his physical body. "It's impossible to know whether an animal I'm communicating with is alive or not," says Dawn.

Some communicators, however, report that they can gain information as to whether the animal is alive. In one instance, Susan Goldstein thought that her Doberman Pinscher, Emily, was lost. Emily had asked to go out in the middle of the night, during a terrible snowstorm. As is their custom, Susan and her husband Bob waited at the door while Emily did her business in their rural yard. "We let her out and she never came back," recalls Susan. Susan and Bob learned later that Emily had suffered from gastric torsion, brought on by eating a toxic substance. She asked to go out to try to find some relief but ended up collapsing and dying on their driveway. Due to the driving snow, her body was immediately covered in a drift.

Susan looked for Emily for two days. Then she called a psychic to ask if she could find Emily. The psychic told her that Emily had died and even told her where her body was. "I negated that information," says Susan. "I wasn't ready to accept it." She didn't even follow up on the information. But, finally, they found Emily's body right where the psychic said it would be. That experience clinched Susan's faith in animal communication.

Sharon Callahan, who herself had a life-transforming near-death experience in which she left her own body, understands the difference between being in the physical body and being out of it. Because of this, she has the ability to tell fairly easily whether an animal is still alive. When she does err, Sharon believes that she senses a similar situation, such as a near-death or severe trauma, that can replicate the out-of-body feeling.

Chapter 12

You Can Talk to the Animals Too

....

The ability to communicate telepathically with animals is not a mysterious gift bestowed on a lucky few. It's something that's innately available to everyone, animal communicators emphatically say. "This is an unexplored part of all of us," says Ginny Debbink. "It is not strange or unusual. It's just something that Western society has cut off."

Talking to the animals is a matter of opening yourself up to the possibility, quieting your mind, opening your heart and making the connection. It sounds simple, and it is. "Anyone who has a desire to do this and is willing to open themselves to it will do it," says Gail De Sciose. But it's easier said than done; each of us has to fight against a lifetime of societal dismissal of our intuitive powers.

If you have any doubts about whether you can do it, here's information right from the horse's mouth. When Susan Rifkin Ajamian's horse, Richie, addressed the topic, through Anita Curtis, he said, "Practice makes everything better. People have to remember that we animals communicate all the time. Species is no barrier. The only ones with a shield are the people. When they lower their shield, they can talk like we do."

LEARNING THROUGH WORKSHOPS

Most of the animal communicators I interviewed for this book devote a good portion of their time training others to communicate with animals. Dawn Hayman reflects the sentiments of many of the other communicators when she says, "My goal is for other people to find their own connection with their animals, for them to be able to do it themselves." Gail De Sciose doesn't think of her workshops as teaching sessions per se. "It is not so much teaching as empowering," she says.

Going to an animal communication workshop taught by a professional communicator is a great way to gain exposure to your own telepathic abilities. I've been to two workshops myself, one sponsored by Anita Curtis and the other sponsored by Dawn Hayman. I can attest to the power of the atmosphere of a workshop. You're in a safe, trusting environment, being taught by a very knowledgeable person, and typically you're able to get validation for the communications you receive. It's a great way to get started, a powerful, mind-expanding experience. Consult the resources section of this book to learn about communicators who offer workshops.

TEACH YOURSELF

If you don't live in an area where a workshop will be sponsored any time soon (and, at this time, most of them seem to be offered on the coasts), you can certainly try animal communication on your own. Follow the steps in this chapter and see if you can make a connection with an animal, either one of your own or one you don't even know. Keep in mind that it doesn't happen instantly. Like learning any new skill, tapping into your telepathic abilities whenever you want takes practice.

YOU'RE ALREADY COMMUNICATING WITH ANIMALS

You may be surprised to learn that you and your animals are already communicating telepathically with one another. "You hear them all the time, you just don't realize it," Dawn Hayman says.

Have you ever had a feeling that your dog needed to go out? Then you offer him the opportunity and he jumps at the chance to go out and relieve himself? He was probably pleading with you silently.

Do you sometimes find yourself walking over to stroke your cat without even thinking about it? He may have beckoned you telepathically.

Dawn urges you to start taking note of those moments. "Start listening to what you say to your animals when you talk to them," she suggests. "Nine times out of ten you are answering them."

I know that I'm always saying out loud what I imagine Kramer and Scout are thinking. I'm starting to realize that maybe they're actually communicating those thoughts and feelings to me and I'm not making them up at all.

Animal communicators say that it's not unusual for them to relate an animal's response to a question and have the client say, "That's what I thought" or "I had a feeling that was true." The clients are already receiving the information from their animals. They may not realize it, or if they do, they probably don't trust their ability to understand yet.

"Because animal communication is so deceptively simple, you tend to look past it," says Dawn. "It isn't difficult. Your biggest stumbling block is thinking you can never do this. You're already doing it."

Dawn makes it sound easy. But Sharon Callahan says that it takes a special person who is willing to put in the time and practice so as to learn to do it effectively. "Everyone can do it," she says. "It simply requires a lot more dedication and work than most people think. Just like learning anything." She acknowledges that, as in other fields, some people have a greater aptitude for telepathic communication and might be able to do it with less effort. For others, a concerted effort to still the mind and open the heart may be required.

A Word About Diet

Penelope Smith and her followers assert that what we consume can play a role in how well we can communicate telepathically. Alcohol, sugar and caffeine inhibit our abilities to receive. Avoid consuming these inhibiting (albeit sometimes pleasurable) substances when you are planning an animal communication session.

Anita Curtis advises drinking a lot of water. Anita told participants at the workshop I attended that when one communicates with animals, toxins build up in your system, and the water will help flush them out.

STARTING OFF ON THE RIGHT FOOT

A few caveats before we start.

- Acknowledge the intelligence and emotions of animals. In order to successfully communicate with animals, you must get past the notion (one that's been ingrained into most of us throughout our lives) that animals are somehow inferior to humans, that they don't think or feel. It may sound obvious, but it bears stating explicitly: Regarding animals as sentient beings with opinions and emotions is essential for successfully communicating with them.

- Don't set yourself up for failure. In a sense, learning to communicate with animals is like learning a new language. You don't expect to be fluent in a foreign language after just one lesson. It takes exposure to the language and lots of practice. So take faith in the glimmers you get at first and keep practicing to hone your skills.

- Don't second-guess yourself. The biggest barrier to learning to communicate is not trusting that what you receive is coming from the animal. I know firsthand how easy it is to assume that that little voice in your head is your "imagination." Rather than discounting a sensation you might feel in your body, try to tune into the feeling and take it on faith that it is coming from the animal.

PENELOPE SMITH'S TECHNIQUES

As a pioneer in the field of animal communication, Penelope Smith has trained many of the professional communicators working today. Many of them are trained to teach her basic workshop. There are, therefore, strong similarities among the techniques that many communicators teach. All the techniques, for example, hinge on quieting the mind and focusing on the animal. Without this clarity of concentration, animal communication is difficult, if not impossible.

Of course there are also many communicators who were not taught by Penelope. Among all the communicators I spoke with, remarkable similarities emerge in terms of the techniques they teach.

The techniques taught by Penelope Smith and her former students (now teachers), follow. This information is gleaned from conversations with Penelope and those communicators I interviewed who had trained with her or her students: Anita Curtis, Gail De Sciose, Ginny Debbink and Dawn Hayman. More detailed information came from Penelope's *Animal Talk*.

After taking you through these steps, I'll introduce you to alternate techniques taught by some of the other communicators I interviewed: Sonya Fitzpatrick, Lydia Hiby, Patty Summers and Sharon Callahan.

Read through the various techniques and decide for yourself which ones to try. Start with the method that resonates most with you. I'd advise giving them all a test-run and then practicing the technique with which you are most comfortable or successful.

Step One: Quiet Your Mind and Observe Your Animal

In our busy daily lives it's sometimes hard to grab even a few minutes of silence. But quiet is an essential component of being able to communicate with animals.

Penelope recommends taking some time with your animal, in a peaceful environment, and sitting quietly with him. Try to still your mind, and look at your animal friend quietly. Sit and gently regard him, focusing softly on him (don't stare). Do this until you feel very calm, and very relaxed, with as clear a mind as you can manage.

Dawn Hayman acknowledges that clearing your mind can be a very difficult task. Rather, she suggests, you should try to listen to your thoughts. In doing so, you might even pick up some communication coming from your animal. "Periodically, you pick things up randomly," she says.

As you sit with your animal, try to become aware of his whole being. As your busy thoughts of the day fade away, you have a chance to regard your animal friend with new eyes. If you find that this isn't happening, don't fret. Be patient. (As Penelope Smith writes, "This isn't a recipe for instant mashed potatoes!")

Practice this basic exercise frequently. Try to do it on a daily basis, even if just for a few minutes.

As you practice, you'll eventually experience a heightened awareness of your animal, a closer connection. You will find yourself more receptive to his feelings, emotions and thoughts.

"Get yourself into a state where you're really receptive," says Penelope. "You're quiet, you're listening, you're not distracted."

Penelope explains that this first step is essential for cultivating your animal communication skills. "It is what makes it safe for an animal to open up to you and feel that you are listening and can understand," she writes in *Animal Talk*. "As you go on to the next steps, be sure and have this step in place as your foundation."

Step Two: Send Your Message

Make sure that you have your animal's attention. Call his name, or give him a rub, whatever it takes to get his attention. Your animal doesn't have to be looking right into your eyes. Just be aware that he's aware of you and that he's listening. You don't have to be looking at someone to be listening to them, and neither does your animal.

Choose a quiet time to communicate. You don't want to interrupt your animal's meal, for example, or try communicating with him while he's barking at a strange sound or batting a toy around. Be focused and attentive together.

You can send your message either silently or out loud. Just make sure it's clear. Try not to send mixed messages by thinking one thing and picturing another because animals sense both pictures and words. You don't want to confuse your animal, particularly at the outset.

In *Animal Talk*, Penelope Smith recommends the following procedure for sending a message (follow each step in sequence):

1. Visualize something. Just create a mental picture.

2. Visualize something and send it to the air a few feet in front of your body.

3. Visualize something and send it to a point in the room—to a bookshelf, for example.

4. Visualize something and send it to your animal's body. You can also verbally describe what you're sending.

5. Get your animal's attention.

6. Say hello.

7. Picture a simple wish or image your animal friend might be interested in, match your words to the mental image and send the message. Repeat until you feel like you're getting across. Vary the images so your animal doesn't get bored and tune out.

If you find yourself having difficulty with this step, you may be distracted. If that's the case, going back to step one might help you get into a more quiet and receptive mode so that you can focus on your animal friend.

Step Three: Receive a Message in Return

You've now sent a message to your animal friend. How do you know he's received it? When you sense a response from him.

Penelope suggests sending the word "hello" and imagining a "hello" in response. It doesn't matter whether you're actually receiving the greeting. Simply by being able to imagine that you are, you are opening your mind up to the possibility, she writes in *Animal Talk*.

Now ask, "How are you?" You should get an answer instantly. It may or may not come in words. It might be a feeling, an emotion, an image or idea. Be open to it and take it. Try to trust your ability to receive a response.

Resist the temptation to automatically invalidate what you receive by discounting it or coming up with a more "rational" way you would know that information. Even if the response (to this or any other question) makes no sense to you now, it might at a future date. Try to keep your own thoughts out of it.

Be sure to acknowledge whatever your animal has communicated. Smile at him, or say "okay" just to let him know you've received it. Most of us don't like it when we don't receive any response from someone that we're speaking with. Your animal friend deserves that same courtesy.

If you need to, go ahead and ask the question a second time. Or ask it in a different way. It can't hurt to ask, but don't get tedious.

Your animal may wish to relay something completely unrelated to your question. Be open to it and respond to it. If you think how long your animal companion has waited for you to listen to him, it's quite possible that he's burning with something to tell you. Acknowledge his message and address his concerns. Then get back to the original question if you'd like.

Once you are satisfied that your original question has been answered, ask your animal friend if he has anything he wants to tell you. Give him the chance to speak his piece.

Keep practicing, with this animal friend or others.

What Type of Message Will You Receive?

Different communicators receive messages in different ways. You might hear words or other sounds; you might feel emotions. You might see images or smell aromas or odors. You might just get a feeling.

The animal sends you everything, says Penelope. You receive what you are open to receiving. As your skills at animal communication develop, you will receive in more senses. "We receive in the sensory channel that's open to us," Penelope says. "When you're really open, you receive all of it."

It's a matter of opening up your internal senses, she says. "Telepathy is like internal sensing; it's receiving on a finer energetic level. You experience it through your body, internally, when you're receiving."

Keep a Journal

Penelope suggests taking notes as you practice your communication. "Keep a journal—that often helps you to get past the doubt that you're doing it because it validates what you're getting," she says. If you notice that your animal friend's behavior changes after a communication, jot that information down in your journal. "You note those things and that helps make it tangible."

Gail De Sciose did just that when she was starting out in animal communication. She made an effort to communicate with at least one animal every day. And she kept a journal. The body of evidence in Gail's journal helped convince her she was actually communicating.

LYDIA HIBY'S BODY SCAN

Lydia Hiby began working as an animal communicator in 1982. Her mentor was a pioneer in the field of animal communication, Beatrice Lydecker. In her book, *Conversations with Animals* (co-written with Bonnie S. Weintraub), Lydia outlines the method for animal communication that she teaches in her workshops.

Lydia's method, like Penelope's, starts with quieting your mind, asking the animal some basic questions and opening yourself up to the responses.

One aspect of her method, the body scan, is uniquely hers. The body scan enables the communicator to feel the physical sensations that the animal is feeling in his body. Lydia discusses the body scan in detail in *Conversations with Animals,* but I'll summarize it here.

After you've had some success with asking the animal questions and receiving responses, you're ready for the body scan. This will provide valuable clues as to how the animal is feeling physically. Lydia includes the body scan in every communication she does, usually saving it for the end of the conversation, after she's gained the animal's trust.

Start by asking the animal, "How are you feeling physically?" Then focus on his head. Ask, "How is your head feeling?" Proceed down the body asking about various body areas as you move along. As you do this, you will feel in your own body what the animal is feeling in his. Your hands substitute for his front paws and your feet for his back paws. Your arms are his front legs and so forth. If the animal has a tail, you'll have sensations where your tail would be.

Before you begin a body scan, take stock of how you are feeling that day, physically, so that you don't mistake your own aches and pains for those of the animal. Remember that you are doing this from "inside" the animal's body, not from your visual perspective. In other words, sensations in your right arm reflect those in his right front leg.

Lydia recommends doing this on a weekly basis with your own animal and keeping a journal. That written record might help your veterinarian if a problem should arise that needs diagnosis.

Lydia advises emphatically that you keep working with the information that you receive, rather than wondering about what you're not getting.

Once you're finished with the body scan, tell the animal that any physical problem you may have sensed should remain with him. In this way, you'll make sure that you don't take on the animal's physical problems.

Lydia advises that you continue to practice communicating with animals in order to hone your skills, but cautions you against overdoing it. Animal communication can be draining work (and animals tend to have short attention spans), so be sure and pace yourself. Fifteen minutes is a good amount of time for a practice session.

SUGGESTIONS FROM PATTY SUMMERS

Patty Summers was not trained by Penelope Smith, though the methods she outlines in her book, *Talking with the Animals*, are nearly identical to Penelope's. In her book, Patty summarizes some basic steps to assist you in telepathic communication:

- Respect all life.
- Believe in your own ability to communicate telepathically with animals.
- Center or quiet yourself. Take a few deep breaths; practice meditation.
- Give your animal friend your full attention. Be mindful in the moment and attentive to the being you are communicating with.
- Picture your question or communication in your mind's eye.
- Send that picture or question mentally to your friend.
- Relax and accept whatever communication you receive, whether it is a thought, idea, feeling or image.
- Acknowledge that you received the communication. Thank your animal friend.

SONYA FITZPATRICK'S TESTS

In her book, *What the Animals Tell Me*, Sonya Fitzpatrick recommends several little tests to help convince you that your message is getting through to your animal friend. She has one for dogs and one for cats.

Just as the other communicators recommend, Fitzpatrick suggests that you put yourself into a state of relaxation. She recommends going to a quiet place and relaxing one part of your body at a time, starting with your feet and moving upward. She says that you should make sure that your animal isn't distracted. If he's asleep, that's fine. But he shouldn't be busy playing, scratching or the like.

For Dogs

Once you're relaxed, mentally envision taking your dog for a walk. Picture yourself taking the leash out, clipping it to your dog's collar, going out the door and proceeding on an enjoyable walk. Once you've pictured the scenario in its full richness, mentally send it to your dog. Chances are good that he will immediately run to you to go for a walk.

Fitzpatrick cautions that you shouldn't try this exercise unless you're willing to follow through with the promise. You don't want to give your dog any reason to distrust your telepathic messages.

For Cats

Because cats don't respond as well to the prospect of going out on a leash, Fitzpatrick recommends that you envision feeding your cat something delicious, such as a can of tuna. Mentally take out the can opener, open the can, smell the aroma of the tuna and put it in your cat's bowl. Think about how delicious it is and how much your cat will enjoy it. Then send the picture you've just painted to your cat. Don't be surprised if he jumps into your lap and asks for some tuna.

Sonya cautions that this might not work on the first try. Don't be disheartened. Continue trying, at different times, until you make that connection.

SHARON CALLAHAN'S EMPHASIS ON MEDITATION

"Animals are talking all the time," says Sharon Callahan, "but you simply can't attune to them until you get very quiet and practice some sort of meditation or contemplative prayer."

Sharon says that learning to meditate is the single most important thing you need to do on your road to learning to communicate with animals. She recommends that you take a meditation class before attending an animal communication workshop.

As you meditate, "become aware that your mind is used to swinging between the past and the future," she writes in "Keys to Inter-species Communication Part 2—From the Commonplace to the

Divine," an article that appeared in both *Species Link* and *Directions Magazine.*

> Even though the movement of thoughts seems so quick, there are gaps in between like the gaps between frames of a strip of movie film. Train yourself to notice the interval between the thoughts instead of the thoughts themselves. Between the thoughts is an interval of silence. In that silence you are out of time. In that non-time, true communion takes place. With dedication you will expand your ability to stay in that interval between thoughts and for a while you will be free. Cultivate that silent freedom.

In addition to meditating, Sharon offers the following advice in her article for those who wish to communicate telepathically with animals. Emphasizing that learning to communicate requires a dedication to practice—and, in some cases, even a lifestyle change—she eschews step-by-step lessons in communication techniques in favor of suggestions for ways you can make changes in the way you look at the world and live your life.

She suggests these exercises as a way to foster the dedication and discipline that she sees as a prerequisite to communicating telepathically with animals.

- Practice listening: When you look at something, such as a flower or an animal, simply look at it, without naming it or classifying it. "When you name, or classify or define, you are no longer listening. It sounds simple, but it is one of the most difficult things and it is the absolute prerequisite to interspecies communication." Sharon emphasizes that humans are always filling their minds with ideas and theories and thinking ahead to the next thing. But if we're doing this, we're not listening. "Nothing can flow into a space that is already full," she writes. She suggests practicing listening every day, which will help you expand your ability to listen.

- Simplify your life: "The simpler you keep your life the easier it will be to listen," writes Sharon. She suggests that you resolve issues as they come up, and let go of things that you do not need to attend to. She further recommends getting rid of your television and halting your magazine and newspaper subscriptions. "The more you do this, the more you disconnect from collective consciousness and re-connect to cosmic consciousness," she says.

- Make a promise not to gossip: If you stop gossiping, you can free up all manner of space in your life, says Sharon. "In the space that is left by the absence of gossiping, you will find stillness and in the stillness you will find communion with your true friends: the animals, the plants, the trees, the sky and the wind."

- Eliminate activities not in alignment with your higher purpose: Everyday activities (going to movies, traveling, and the like) might be enjoyable, but do they further you along on your spiritual path? Sharon suggests that you try to limit your activities to those that feed your soul and support your desire to listen, to simplify, to not gossip and to attune silently to other beings.

- In all things move away from separation toward unity, away from contraction toward expansion: You may feel that you are separating yourself from the rest of the world by simplifying your life and eliminating activities that don't serve your higher purpose. But Sharon says that you are only separating yourself from things in this world in favor of uniting yourself with the divine. You're moving from smallness to expansiveness. "It takes courage, desire, dedication, discipline and faith to simplify life so that you may truly listen to that which is real," she writes.

- Be joyful and have fun: Delight in being alive, suggests Sharon. "Nature and animals are filled with joy; be joyful too."

LEARNING TO TRUST

Regardless of the technique you choose to practice for connecting with animals, you'll inevitably have to get over the hurdle of learning to trust that you're actually communicating. Sonya Fitzpatrick's tests are a great way to get validation right at the beginning that you're actually communicating telepathically with your animal. But try not to test your animal's patience with simple tasks too much, says Dawn. Resist the temptation to tell him, "If you understand me, lie down." Chances are, she says, after your animal lies down, you'll decide it was just a coincidence. And you'll ask him to do something else. And then yet another task. "They know you can hear them," says Dawn. "And it is natural for them to resent being asked to do parlor tricks."

Penelope Smith agrees. "They get really tired of that really fast, though they'll usually do it for beginners." Although your animal might bend over backwards at first, after a while he'll look up at you and say, "You must be joking," says Penelope.

One way to tell that you're getting through to your own animal is the subtle shift in the animal. "Generally you see the difference in them; you see the difference in the quality of your relationship; you see the way they relate to you is different," says Penelope.

Even if you're convinced that your animal is receiving your messages, how can you tell whether you're correctly receiving communication from your animal friend in return?

Unfortunately, there's no easy test for that. And therein lies the most difficult part for people who are just starting out in animal communication: Trusting that what they receive is actually coming from the animal.

It's not just the beginners who have doubts. "There isn't a day that goes by that I don't think, 'What if I can't do this?,'" says Lydia Hiby. Dawn Hayman echoed those thoughts when she told me, "The doubt never goes away. I still question it when it comes to my own animals." At the workshop I attended led by Anita Curtis, a participant asked her, "Do you ever get to the point where you trust yourself?" Anita's response: "Not yet."

That said, both Patty Summers and Lydia Hiby mention that after a great deal of experience you'll learn to differentiate between your imagination and actual communication. "Eventually you start being able to tell when it is not coming from you," says Patty. "It doesn't feel like your energy."

Keep practicing and you will receive validation, especially if you're speaking with animals that aren't yours. It's that validation that's essential to build up your confidence and your trust in yourself.

For this reason, many animal communicators advise talking to animals other than those you live with. "It's always easier to talk to animals that aren't yours," says Dawn. With your own animal companions, you have an emotional investment in their responses to your questions. You might be hoping for a specific response, so when you get it, you chalk it up to wishful thinking.

When you're speaking with other animals and have no stake in the response, it's easier to believe. And when the animal tells you something about his life that you would have no way of knowing (and then his person confirms the truth of the statement), you get that all-important validation.

Remember that you're talking to an animal, and not a person. "It's easier to trust the animals because humans tell you what you want to hear," says Nancy Mueller.

"Not having the validation makes it difficult," says Lydia Hiby. "At first your rational mind kicks in and you don't want to believe it's coming from the animal." Lydia advises stepping outside of yourself. Take your own thoughts out of the equation and allow your first impression to be correct. "Trusting your feelings, for some people, is a very scary place to go."

This difficulty in trusting that you're communicating is understandable. "We are taught so consistently throughout our lives that this isn't possible," says Ginny Debbink. "We are trained not to trust. It's a lifelong training and it takes a lot of work to get past that." Dawn agrees. "We are socialized to invalidate ourselves right and left," she says.

If you receive conflicting messages from the animal, if he contradicts himself from one session to the next, for example, don't automatically invalidate either response. "Their opinions change, just like humans'," says Dawn.

Patty Summers advises treating yourself gently. "Play with it," she suggests. "Quit putting so much pressure on yourself. It is just information." If you get the sense that your animal would like his bed moved to the other side of the room, she advises, just try it and see what happens. "Most people first connect through a gut or inner knowing," she says. "They'll say, 'I had a funny feeling.'"

The doubts are natural, says Penelope. They come up as part of the learning process. "Keep practicing and you'll see the results." Dawn echoes those sentiments. "The biggest thing to do is to keep trying—let it come," says Dawn.

Like the other communicators, Patty suggests jotting down what you receive. That written record can be validating in and of itself (at least you're getting something, right?). And you never know when something will happen that will confirm what you received. Having written it down when it's fresh in your mind, it's there for you in black and white to consult when you need it.

SETTING BOUNDARIES

If you're talking with an animal who is ill or in pain, you may feel that pain in your own body. It's important for you not to retain that pain——you don't want to suffer negative effects from your communication. "I ask that information be given to me in a less primary way, rather than feeling the physical pain," says Alice McClure. You can also do what Lydia suggests and tell the animal that any physical problem he has should remain with him.

Once you open your telepathic channels, will you be bombarded by communicating animals all of the time? Not if you don't let that happen, says Penelope. You can't remain open 24 hours a day, 7 days a week, she cautions. "When I train people, I tell them not to invite a

131

constant stream, or they'll just be overwhelmed. Open 24 hours? Wait a minute, let's be sensible."

THE WORKSHOP EXPERIENCE

Attending a workshop can really help you make inroads in building that trust in your own ability to communicate telepathically. The first time I tried communicating telepathically was at Anita Curtis' workshop. I'd been sent to the workshop by *Pets: part of the family* magazine for an article I was writing. I was a true neophyte and had never even considered that I might have the ability to communicate with animals.

I believed that animal communication was possible—I was certain that Ginny Debbink, the communicator who had spoken with Kramer and Scout, could do it. But I had no expectation that I'd succeed.

One of the first exercises we did was to pair off and take turns sending a mental image to our partner. First, Anita had one person in each pair visualize a specific color. Then she had us formulate an image of an object in that color and send it. You could have knocked me over with a feather when I received the green pine tree that my partner had sent me.

We moved on to communicating with the animals of our fellow workshop participants. In this workshop, we brought photographs of our animal friends, not the actual animal. My first partner had a driving horse he wanted me to speak with. He wanted to know how Rose felt about her job, pulling a carriage with a partner.

When I asked her about her job, I felt sensations that she would feel as she worked, a breeze on my face, the cold metal of the bit in my mouth, the rhythm of the hooves. Then I asked her how she liked her work and these words popped into my head: "I like it, but it's hard." I inquired about her partner and all I got was a feeling of dead weight on my left side.

Of course this didn't mean anything to me, but I related it to Rose's person. His eyes lit up. It turns out that Rose's partner, who works on her left, is a slacker who, literally, doesn't pull his own weight. Rose has to do 75 perecnt of the work. So naturally she would feel dead weight on her left. My partner was sure I had actually connected. I was elated.

Next I spoke with Tracie, the American Eskimo dog of another workshop participant. I asked her what she liked to do and immediately got the sense of her rubbing her head under my chin and along my neck, rather like a cat does. This seemed like an odd activity for a dog, but I related it to the partner and learned that indeed Tracie does do that all of the time.

The workshop did a wonderful job of bolstering my confidence about my own abilities. I mention it here not to brag in any way, but to illustrate how someone who thought she had absolutely no innate abilities to communicate telepathically was flush with success at the end of a one-day workshop. If you have the opportunity to attend a workshop, I strongly urge you to do so. It'll be an unforgettable experience.

LEAVE YOUR EGO AT THE DOOR

If you succeed in tapping into your ability to communicate with animals, remember to set your ego aside. "It is important for animal communicators to view themselves as a conduit," says Ginny Debbink. If you are talking with someone else's animal on her behalf, you serve as an interpreter of what the two parties have to say to one another. It is not for you to interject your own judgments into the conversation.

"Being good at this means that you have to spiritually grow and get into an open space of awareness and listening," says Penelope Smith. There's no room for judging or following your own agenda. "You'll be slapped in the face if you're putting your own agenda into it. The people won't like it and the animals won't like it."

Tact and diplomacy in relating information is very important. "You must be truthful, but you don't have to be brutal," says Anita Curtis.

If you find yourself offering to communicate with animals for others, be sure and review Penelope Smith's Code of Ethics for Interspecies Telepathic Communicators found in Appendix B of this book. It will give you important guidelines on ethical behavior that are crucial in this very personal work.

LIFE-CHANGING WORK

No matter how you get there, if you are able to open up and successfully communicate telepathically with animals, it will almost surely be life changing.

Perhaps you'll feel like Ginny Debbink, who told me, "The whole journey has been one of the most powerful things in my life. It has totally changed my life."

It will change not only your life, but your animals' lives too. "They really appreciate it when you communicate," says Penelope Smith. "It really enhances their life and connection with you."

Don't be surprised if your perspective on the world is turned upside down once you begin to see it through the eyes of other species. "It is crucial in our evolution as spirits and souls to open up to other species," Penelope says. "There are vast repercussions to the changes in the people and life around them from opening up to this," says Penelope, who has seen these changes personally as she's trained thousands of people in interspecies telepathic communication. "It is just so beautiful, I devote my whole life to it."

Appendix A

Resources

··

ANIMAL COMMUNICATORS

The animal communicators interviewed for this book follow. All are available for consultations except as noted.

Sharon Callahan
Anaflora
P.O. Box 1056
Mt. Shasta, CA 96067
Phone: 530-926-6424
Fax: 530-926-1245
www.anaflora.com

Anita Curtis★
P.O. Box 182
Gilbertsville, PA 19525-0182
Phone: 610-327-3820
Fax: 610-970-2696
www.anitacurtis.com

Gail De Sciose★
P.O. Box 6697
New York, NY 10128
212-388-7319

Ginny Debbink★
51 Schooley's Mt. Rd.
Long Valley, NJ 07853
908-876-9442
debbink@interpow.net

Sonya Fitzpatrick★
10706 Timberwagon Circle
The Woodlands, TX 77380
281-364-0608
www.petvoice.com

Dawn Hayman★
3364 State Rt. 12
Clinton, NY 13323
315-737-9339
www.springfarmcares.org

Lydia Hiby★
10932 Arleta Ave.
Mission Hills, CA 91345
818-365-4647
www.lydiahiby.com

Alice Gail McClure
2565 CR35
Norwood, NY 13668
315-353-2990
mcclure@northnet.org

Nancy Mueller
Fair Chance Farm
261 Randolph Rd.
Freehold, NJ 07728
732-780-2202

Penelope Smith★ +
P.O. Box 1060
Point Reyes, CA 94956
415-663-1247
penelope@svn.net
www.animaltalk.net

To order books and tapes directly: 800-356-9315

Patty Summers★
P.O. Box 275
Evington, VA 24550
804-821-3612
mail@psanimalcommunications.com
www.psanimalcommunications.com

★ gives workshops
+ not available for consultations

RECOMMENDED RESOURCES
Books

Curtis, Anita. *Animal Wisdom: How to Hear the Animals.* iUniverse, 2000.

Fitzpatrick, Sonya with Patricia Burkhart Smith. *What the Animals Tell Me: Understanding Your Pet's Complex Emotions.* Hyperion, 1998.

Hiby, Lydia, with Bonnie S. Weintraub. *Conversations with Animals: Cherished Messages and Memories as Told by an Animal Communicator.* NewSage Press, 1998.

Myers, Arthur. *Communicating with Animals: The Spiritual Connection Between People and Nature.* NTC/Contemporary Publishing, 1997.

Sheldrake, Rupert. *Dogs That Know When Their Owners Are Coming Home and Other Unexplained Powers of Animals: An Investigation.* Crown Publishers, 1999.

Smith, Penelope. *Animal Talk: Interspecies Telepathic Communication.* Beyond Words Publishing, 1999.

Smith, Penelope. *When Animals Speak: Advanced Interspecies Communication.* Beyond Words Publishing, 1999.

Summers, Patty. *Talking with the Animals.* Hampton Roads Publishing Company, 1998.

Newsletters

Curtis, Anita. *Animal Channel.* www.anitacurtis.com, 610-327-3820.

Smith, Penelope. *Species Link—The Journal of Interspecies Telepathic Communication.* www.animaltalk.net; Pegasus Publications, P.O. Box 1060, Point Reyes, CA 94956, 415-663-1247.

Audiotapes

Johnson, Katrene and Ginny Debbink. *Opening to the Animals: A Self-Hypnosis Approach to Communicating with Animals.* Flying Dog Press, www.flyingdogpress.com, 1-800-7-FLY-DOG.

Forty-five minutes with detailed users guide.

Smith, Penelope. *Animal Death: A Spiritual Journey.* www.animaltalk.net, 800-356-9315.

Ninety minutes.

Smith, Penelope. *The Interspecies Telepathic Connection Tape Series.* www.animaltalk.net, 800-356-9315.

Six hours.

Summers, Patty. *Animal Communication.* www.psanimalcommunications. com, 804-821-3612.

> Contains introduction to animal communication and meditations and steps.

Videotapes

"Stories Of Animal Communication," with Dawn Hayman. Spring Farm CARES, www.springfarmcares.org, 315-737-9339.

"Telepathic Communication with Animals," produced by Kelly Hart/Hartworks. www.animaltalk.net, 800-356-9315.

> Featuring Penelope Smith. Forty-six minutes.

"The Psychic Connection." Anita Curtis, www.anitacurtis.com, 610-327-3820.

> Featuring interviews with a variety of animal communicators, including Anita Curtis, Lydia Hiby, Penelope Smith.

Web sites

Penelope Smith's Directory of Interspecies Telepathic Communicators.

http://www.animaltalk.net

Appendix B

Code of Ethics for Interspecies Telepathic Communicators

••

Our motivation is compassion for all beings and a desire to help all species understand each other better, particularly to help restore the lost human ability to freely and directly communicate with other species.

We honor those that come to us for help, not judging, condemning, or invalidating them for their mistakes or misunderstanding but honoring their desire for change and harmony.

We know that to keep this work as pure and harmonious as possible requires that we continually grow spiritually. We realize that telepathic communication can be clouded or overlaid by our own unfulfilled emotions, critical judgments, or lack of love for self and others. We walk in humility, willing to recognize and clear up our own errors in understanding others' communication (human and non-human alike).

We cultivate knowledge and understanding of the dynamics of human, non-human, and interspecies behavior and relationships, to increase the good results of our work. We get whatever education and/or personal help we need to do our work effectively, with compassion, respect, joy, and harmony.

We seek to draw out the best in everyone and increase understanding toward mutual resolution of problems. We go only where we are asked to help, so that others are receptive and we truly can help. We respect the feelings and ideas of others and work for interspecies understanding, not pitting one side against another but walking with compassion for all. We acknowledge the things that we cannot change and continue where our work can be most effective.

We respect the privacy of people and animal companions we work with, and honor their desire for confidentiality. While doing our best to help, we allow others their own dignity and help them to help their animal companions. We cultivate understanding and ability in others, rather than dependence on our ability. We offer people ways to be involved in understanding and growth with their fellow beings of other species.

We acknowledge our limitations, seeking help from other professionals as needed. It is not our job to name and treat diseases, and we refer people to veterinarians for diagnosis of physical illness. We may relay animals' ideas, feelings, pains, symptoms, as they describe them or as we feel or perceive them, and this may be helpful to veterinary health professionals. We may also assist through handling of stresses, counseling, and other gentle healing methods. We let clients decide for themselves how to work with healing their animal companions' distress, disease, or injury, given all the information available.

The goal of any consultation, lecture, workshop, or interspecies experience is more communication, balance, compassion, understanding, and communion among all beings. We follow our heart, honoring the spirit and life of all beings as One.

Formulated in 1990 by Penelope Smith, author and Animal
Communication Specialist. Reprinted with permission.

Index